THE YALE EDITIONS OF THE PRIVATE PAPERS OF JAMES BOSWELL

Boswell's London Journal, 1762–1763

Boswell in Holland, 1763–1764

Portraits by Sir Joshua Reynolds

SIR JOSHUA REYNOLDS, A SELF-PORTRAIT

"The last picture Sir Joshua Reynolds did of himself. It has a sort of *pulled up* look, and not the placid gentleness of his smiling manner; but the features, though rather too largely and strongly limned, are most exactly portrayed; and the dress in every respect being such as he usually wore, I think it the best representation of my celebrated friend."—BOSWELL

PORTRAITS

BY

SIR JOSHUA REYNOLDS

Character Sketches of Oliver Goldsmith, Samuel Johnson, and David Garrick, together with other Manuscripts of Reynolds recently discovered among the Private Papers of James Boswell and now first published

PREPARED FOR THE PRESS WITH
INTRODUCTIONS AND NOTES BY FREDERICK W. HILLES
BODMAN PROFESSOR OF ENGLISH LITERATURE, YALE
UNIVERSITY

WILLIAM HEINEMANN LTD

MELBOURNE : LONDON : TORONTO

* * * * *

The Yale Editions of the Private Papers of James Boswell will consist of two independent but parallel series planned and executed for different types of readers. One, the "research" edition, will give a complete text of Boswell's journals, diaries, and memoranda; of his correspondence; and of "The Life of Johnson", from the original manuscript: the whole running to at least thirty volumes. It will preserve the spelling and capitalisation of the original documents, and will be provided with extensive scholarly annotation. A *large group of* editors and a permanent office staff are engaged in this comprehensive undertaking, the first volume of which may appear by 1955. The other, the reading or "trade" edition, will select from the total mass of papers those portions that appear likely to interest the general reading public, and will present them in modern spelling and with annotation of a popular cast. The publishers may also issue limited de luxe printings of the trade volumes, with extra illustrations and special editorial matter, but in no case will the trade volumes or the de luxe printings include matter from Boswell's archives that will not also appear in the research edition.

The present volume is the third of the trade edition.

FIRST PUBLISHED 1952

PRINTED IN GREAT BRITAIN
AT THE WINDMILL PRESS
KINGSWOOD, SURREY

ADVISORY COMMITTEE

C. A. Malcolm, M.A., PH.D., O.B.E., Librarian to the Society of Writers to the Signet, Edinburgh

Henri Peyre, DR.ÈS L., Sterling Professor of French, Yale University

L. F. Powell, M.A., D.LITT., F.R.S.L., F.L.A., Sometime Librarian of the Taylor Institution, Reviser of Hill's Edition of Boswell's "Life of Johnson"

S. C. Roberts, M.A., Master of Pembroke College, Cambridge

L. W. Sharp, M.A., PH.D., Librarian to the University of Edinburgh

T. B. Simpson, Q.C., LL.D., F.R.S.E., Sheriff of Perth and Angus.

D. Nichol Smith, LITT.D., LL.D., F.B.A., Emeritus Professor of English Literature in the University of Oxford

Chauncey B. Tinker, PH.D., LITT.D., L.H.D., Sterling Professor of English Literature Emeritus, and Keeper of Rare Books in the University Library, Yale University

TABLE OF CONTENTS

LIST OF ILLUSTRATIONS

—

LIST OF ILLUSTRATIONS

LIST OF ILLUSTRATIONS

from the original in the Yale University Library.

"Dear Sir Joshua, even with his inimitable pencil, never drew more interesting, more resembling portraits [than in these dialogues]. I hear them all speak. I see every action, every gesture which accompanied every word. I hear the deep-toned and indignant accents of our friend Johnson; I hear the affected periods of Gibbon; the natural, the easy, the friendly, the elegant language, the polished sarcasm, softened with the sweet temper, of Sir Joshua."

HANNAH MORE.

from the line-engraving by John Hall, 1780.

"The picture . . . painted by Sir J. Reynolds and the prints made from it are as like the original as it is possible to be. When he was introduced to a blind French lady, the servant happening to stretch out her mistress's hand to lay hold of the historian's cheek, she thought upon feeling its rounded contour that some trick was being played upon her with the *sitting* part of a child, and exclaimed, 'Fi donc!' " MALONE.

from an engraving made in 1754 for a new edition of Stow's *Survey of London*.

The spectator is looking north, facing Leicester House, which had been the home of George II when Prince of Wales, and later of his eldest son Frederick, father of George III. The statue in the centre is of George II. In 1760 Reynolds purchased a house in the middle of the block of buildings on the west side, which was his home for the rest of his life. Hogarth lived on the east side of the square.

PREFACE

POPE laughed at those authors who let it be known that they were obliged to publish by "request of friends". But this is a book for which such claims can be made quite truthfully. When, in the autumn of 1946, it became known that among the Boswell Papers there were a number of manuscripts in the hand of Sir Joshua Reynolds, including character sketches of Goldsmith and Garrick, pressure to publish them was brought to bear on Colonel Isham. Later, when the papers became the property of Yale University, similar requests were directed at the Editorial Committee which is charged with the responsibility of publishing the Yale Editions of the Private Papers of James Boswell. This book is designed to satisfy such requests.

The Reynolds papers, discovered in 1940 in a stable-loft at Malahide Castle, comprise, in addition to the Goldsmith and Garrick items, an ironical discourse written for students of the Royal Academy, a fragmentary essay on Shakespeare, two important letters from Reynolds to Boswell, a note from Reynolds to Johnson, and memoranda concerning such topics as painting, gardening, the theatre, literature, and the art of conversation. With these papers were found some interesting notes which Boswell made on the early life of Reynolds. There are also copies of four letters, two from Sir Joshua to Sir William Chambers and two from Boswell to Reynolds, which have been omitted from this volume because they have already appeared in print and to reprint them here would serve no useful purpose. The collection is supplemented by three items which were discovered among the Boswell Papers at Fettercairn House by Professor C. Colleer Abbott: two notes from Reynolds to Boswell and a letter which Reynolds wrote to Bennet Langton.

The chief interest in these papers is the light they throw on the lives of some of the more important members of the Johnsonian circle. When planning this volume we therefore decided to include, in addition to the newly discovered material, Sir Joshua's character sketch of Dr. Johnson and the two dialogues which he wrote to illustrate Johnson's manner of talking. The manuscript of the character sketch is in my possession; that of the dialogues is in the Yale University Library, the gift of the late Gabriel Wells. Although the character sketch of Johnson has been in print for almost a century, the text known to the reading public is inaccurate and incomplete. What is here published is, of course, basically what has already appeared, but is in fact a new text with important additions and corrections. The two dialogues have often been reprinted, but the version included in this volume, based on the manuscript which was sent to the printer, is an improvement over its predecessors. The Johnsonian dialogues and the Johnsonian memoir, here reprinted with the new portraits of Goldsmith and Garrick, support Malone's statement that analysis of character was Sir Joshua's amusement, that "his close study of the characters of men, for which he was remarkable, proceeded chiefly from the delight he felt in considering man under all his varieties".

The editorial practice adopted in *Boswell's London Journal* and *Boswell in Holland* has been followed in this book; what Sir Joshua wrote, as well as all quotations from other manuscripts or books, has been modernised. Spellings conform to the house style of the printers; punctuation and capitalisation have been normalised. Editorial insertions are marked by square brackets, and obvious slips of the pen have been silently corrected. There is no doubt that this policy would have had Sir Joshua's blessing. Textual matters peculiar to the printers or writers of the eighteenth or nineteenth centuries may be likened to costume. And Sir Joshua constantly reminded his students that the dress was not part of the man. It is, said he, "only an amusement for an antiquarian; and if it obstructs the general design of the piece, it is to be disregarded by the artist."

Some readers may wonder why the illustrations in this book are based not on the original paintings but on contemporary engravings.

The answer is simple. The engraving was normally done under the supervision of Reynolds and done when the colours were still fresh, before the portrait had deteriorated. It may sound like a paradox, but illustrations which derive from a good contemporary engraving are closer to the original than are modern photographs of the original painting. The design on the title-page is drawn from the seal which Sir Joshua stamped on each of the drawings and prints in his own collection.

It is a pleasure to acknowledge the assistance that I have received from a number of people. The generous gift of Mr. Paul Mellon helped to bring the papers to Yale and thus made them available for publication. I have gladly adopted some of the suggestions which Colonel Isham made to me when I first had the privilege of going over the manuscripts with him. My friend Mr. Arthur A. Houghton, Jr., will recognise, I hope with pleasure, the contribution which he has made. Dr. Robert F. Metzdorf has read the proofs, and Dr. Marshall Waingrow, who has read the book before and after it was in type, has prepared the index. I have the uneasy feeling that I have forgotten many who have patiently answered my questions. Those that I can name are Mr. James M. Osborn and Professors Christopher M. Dawson, Louis A. Landa, Ralph M. Wardle, and William K. Wimsatt. But my chief thanks are due to the members of the Editorial Committee, who have read and discussed this book in its various stages, and to Mrs. Marion S. Pottle, whose careful work in cataloguing the thousands of documents in the Boswell Papers has given her a knowledge of the contents of that collection which is unrivalled.

F.W.H.

Yale University, New Haven
5 May 1952

I

SIR JOSHUA

§ 1

"SIR JOSHUA REYNOLDS was on very many accounts one of the most memorable men of his time." This sentence is to be found in the obituary which, we are told, Edmund Burke wrote in Sir Joshua's house a few minutes after his friend's death in 1792. Obituaries cannot always be relied upon. They are closely related to epitaphs, and, as Johnson said, "in lapidary inscriptions a man is not upon oath." But since, in the highly personal letters which Burke was writing to his friends, he was saying of Reynolds much the same sort of thing that he had written for publication, there is no reason to doubt his sincerity. And when it is remembered that no one at this time knew Reynolds better than Burke, the obituary takes on an added importance. A contemporary journalist called it the eulogium of Apelles pronounced by Pericles. It is an account of the father of English painting by one of England's greatest political philosophers.

"He was the first Englishman who added the praise of the elegant arts to the other glories of his country. In taste, in grace, in facility, in happy invention, and in the richness and harmony of colouring, he was equal to the great masters of the renowned ages. In portrait he went beyond them. . . . He possessed the theory as perfectly as the practice of his art. To be such a painter, he was a profound and penetrating philosopher.

"In full affluence of foreign and domestic fame, admired by the expert in art and by the learned in science, courted by the great, caressed by sovereign powers, and celebrated by distinguished poets, his native humility, modesty, and candour never forsook him even on surprise or provocation; nor was the least degree of

B

arrogance or assumption visible to the most scrutinising eye in any part of his conduct or discourse.

"His talents of every kind, powerful from nature and not meanly cultivated by letters, his social virtues in all the relations and all the habitudes of life, rendered him the centre of a very great and unparalleled variety of agreeable societies, which will be dissipated by his death. . . ."

The points which Burke makes—Sir Joshua's extraordinary skill as a painter, his equable disposition, and his faculty for bringing together the outstanding men of his day—are restatements of what others had already said of him in public. Perhaps nowhere are these points made more effectively than in Boswell's dedication to him of the *Life of Johnson*: "Your excellence, not only in the art over which you have long presided with unrivalled fame, but also in philosophy and elegant literature, is well known to the present, and will continue to be the admiration of future ages. Your equal and placid temper, your variety of conversation, your true politeness, by which you are so amiable in private society, and that enlarged hospitality which has long made your house a common centre of union for the great, the accomplished, the learned, and the ingenious: all these qualities I can, in perfect confidence of not being accused of flattery, ascribe to you."

These are the most authoritative remarks made about Reynolds at the close of his life. They reflect the reputation which he had built up for himself not only as a painter but as a prominent member of the society of his time. They are made by men who knew him intimately, and any characterisation of him which differs from these in its main outline and emphases is to be regarded as suspect.

§ 2

At the beginning of 1753, before he was thirty years old, Reynolds had settled in London, which was to be his home for the

February 24. 1792.

Last Night, in the sixty ninth year of his age, died at his
house in Leicester fields, Sr Joshua Reynolds. His illness
was long, but borne with a mild & cheerful fortitude, without
the least mixture of any thing irritable or querulous, agree-
-ably to the placid & even Tenour of his whole Life. He
had from the beginning of his Malady a distinct view of
his Dissolution, which he contemplated with that entire
composure, which nothing but the innocence, integrity, &
usefulness of his Life, & an unaffected submission to
the Will of Providence could bestow. In this situation he
had every consolation from family tenderness, which his
tenderness to his family had always merited.
Sir Joshua Reynolds was ~~a man~~ on very many
accounts one of the most memorable men of his ~~age~~
time. He was the first Englishman who added the
praise of the elegant Arts to the other glories of his Country. In
Taste, in grace, in facility, in ~~pleasing~~ happy invention, & in the
richness & harmony of colouring, he was equal to the great
masters of the renowned Ages. In Portrait he went
beyond them; for he communicated to that description of the

FIRST PAGE OF BURKE'S OBITUARY OF REYNOLDS

"The hand of the great master and the affectionate friend is so visible that it is scarcely necessary to inform the reader that it was written by Mr. Burke, not many hours after the melancholy event which it commemorates."—MALONE

rest of his life. One of eleven children, he was the son of the schoolmaster of Plympton, a pleasant village not far from Plymouth. His formal education had been restricted to what he had learned from his father. Early showing an interest in painting, he had been sent to London to work in the studio of the most fashionable portrait-painter of the day, Thomas Hudson. Then after seven years in his native Devonshire he had spent two years in Italy, where he may be said to have completed his student days. What happened immediately after his return is quite unlike the usual story of a young artist struggling to gain recognition. Almost at once his paintings attracted favourable notice. Within two or three years he had become the most successful portrait-painter in the country. Within eight years he was able to buy a large house in what is now Leicester Square. He set up his coach. He began to assemble a notable collection of Old Masters. He entertained expansively. His fellow painters may have viewed his rise with mixed feelings, but they could not overlook his abilities. He took an active part in the various organisations which preceded the founding of the Royal Academy, and was the obvious person to become its first president, a position which he held until his death.

First and foremost a painter, working long hours in his studio and rarely taking a vacation, Reynolds spent his evenings with those who knew little or nothing about painting. Artists were his associates; his friends were chiefly politicians, men about town, and literary folk. This was no accident. From his early days he was determined to broaden himself. The man who was a painter and nothing else he deplored as a pedant. When he was at the height of his career, he advised the young artist to be a student of human nature. "Reading, if it can be made the favourite recreation of his leisure hours, will improve and enlarge his mind, without retarding his actual industry. What such partial and desultory reading cannot afford, may be supplied by the conversation of learned and ingenious men." As a child Reynolds had come under the influence of Zachariah Mudge, whom Burke was to describe as "a very learned and thinking man and much inclined to philosophy in the spirit of the Platonists". As a young man he developed this philosophical bent, and, as we shall see, it was his manner of thinking that first caught the attention of Samuel Johnson.

The pleasure Reynolds took in the "conversation of learned and ingenious men" accounts for his being the founder of the most famous literary society in history, "The" Club. Johnson, of course, was the dominant figure in this group, but Reynolds was their "Romulus". Reynolds was able to do what Johnson could not do—assemble a gathering which included leaders of society, bishops, statesmen, and authors. No one can forget the names of the most eminent members, but it may be worth while to list some of them, if only to emphasise their standing, not merely in their own time, but in the two centuries that have elapsed since. Reynolds himself was spokesman for the arts. Science was represented by Sir Joseph Banks, President of the Royal Society. Then there were Sir John Hawkins and Dr. Burney, historians of music; Bishop Percy, whose *Reliques* revived an interest in old ballads and revitalised English poetry; Goldsmith, most gifted man of letters of his day, and Sheridan, one of the most brilliant of dramatists; Steevens and Malone, editors of Shakespeare; Charles James Fox, noted for his eloquence; Adam Smith, the father of economics; Garrick, greatest of English actors; Gibbon, most famous of historians; Boswell, supreme among biographers; Burke, unsurpassed as a political philosopher—these and others of almost equal eminence in their time gathered around the bulky figure of Samuel Johnson, who, there as elsewhere, proved his title of Ἄναξ ἀνδρῶν.

But Sir Joshua's circle was far wider than this. Mrs. Thrale writes with asperity that he set himself up as a patron of literature, "so that no book goes rapidly through a first edition now, but the author is at Reynolds's table in a trice." He was a gregarious person and delighted in bringing together a variety of people. His dinners became celebrated. Because of his profession he met all types of men and women. Because of his manners, which were "gentle, complying, and bland", he easily made friendships. Himself a Whig, he was closely associated with extreme Tories. A model of politeness, he gambled with the most notorious rakes of the day. Soon after dining at aristocratic Holland House, he was the guest of the lovely courtesan Nelly O'Brien. (In his engagement book he playfully calls her "My Lady O'Brien".) At his table were to be found gentlemen-adventurers from India, aldermen from the City, clergymen from Ireland, officers of the Royal Navy—"Mediterranean friends as he called them." One day he would associate with the conventional poet-philosopher James Beattie, fresh from Aberdeen; another with the unconventional lampooner Dr. Wolcot ("Peter Pindar"), from the west of England. Among his close friends were hard-headed men of business like Sir William Forbes, the banker, or Philip Metcalfe, the distiller. But he was equally at home in the company of the ribald Laurence Sterne, the dilettante Horace Walpole, or the libertine John Wilkes. It may be doubted whether any man of his time had a wider circle of friends.

§ 3

In appearance Sir Joshua was not impressive. Slight of frame, he was not five feet six in height. His complexion was florid, his features blunt. His face was scarred from the smallpox, which he had had as a child; his upper lip disfigured as the result of a fall from a horse when a young man. Yet no one seems to have considered him ugly. His face combined placidity with great good humour. He was in every sense a sanguine person. His sister Frances, to be sure, thought him "a gloomy tyrant", but this would seem to reflect her own outlook on life rather than his. Both Malone and Burke mention his "strong turn for humour", and the quality frequently stressed by his friends was, as one put it, his "uncommon flow of spirits". Boswell "envied his activity and placid disposition".

Goldsmith's witty verses introduce specific details that must always be a part of Sir Joshua's portrait. Reynolds was an inveterate snuff-taker, carelessly spilling much of it on his waistcoat. And because of deafness he carried an ear-trumpet. Hence the conclusion of Goldsmith's mock epitaph:

To coxcombs averse, yet most civilly steering,
When they judged without skill, he was still hard of
hearing;
When they talked of their Raphaels, Correggios, and stuff,
He shifted his trumpet, and only took snuff.

To take snuff, it should be recalled, could mean *to take umbrage*. Goldsmith suggests that though Reynolds was annoyed at the opinions of fashionable connoisseurs, he suffered in silence.

We hear so much of his politeness in society, of the blandness of his disposition, that we might naturally think of him as a rather colourless member of a conversational group. On this point Madame d'Arblay is most enlightening. He had, she wrote, "a suavity of disposition that set everybody at their ease in his society; though neither that, nor what Dr. Johnson called his *inoffensiveness*, bore the character of a tame insipidity that never differed from a neighbour, or that knew not how to support an opposing opinion with firmness and independence. On the contrary, Sir Joshua was even peculiar in thinking for himself; and frequently, after a silent rumination, to which he was unavoidably led by not following up, from his deafness, the various stages of any given question, he would surprise the whole company by starting some new and unexpected idea on the subject in discussion, in a manner so imaginative and so original, that it either drew the attention of the interlocutors into a quite different mode of argument to that with which they had set out, or it incited them to come forth, in battle array, against the novelty of his assertions. In the first case, he was frankly gratified, but never moved to triumph; in the second, he met the opposition with candour, but was never browbeaten from defending his cause with courage, even by the most eminent antagonist."

This description throws light on one of the Reynolds papers discovered at Malahide Castle. Sir Joshua is commenting on some of his associates and then, it would seem, under the symbol GH is describing himself:

AB, CD, EF, if they cannot be numbered with the wits of the age, they still obtrude themselves into their societies. Though they have no abilities of any sort themselves, they know those that have, and can repeat with accuracy what they have heard fall from them, or what they have read. It is not part of their business to weigh or examine what they hear or read. With them there appears to be no communication of the ears or eyes with the brain; the passages from those organs lead only to the tongue, and there the matter evaporates. They hate argument, reasoning, or discussion of any kind. Anecdote is their delight, of which they are well furnished. Having never learnt the art of thinking, having formed no general principles on any subject, they have no standard to which their anecdotes may refer. They possess crude materials only, but having not the art of using them, of putting things together, they fabricate nothing. Such men are not wiser at the end of sixty years than they were at twenty. Those anecdote-mongers appear promising young men, but remaining in the same state when old, are neglected as silly fellows when old, not possessing even the experience of age.

GH. His character is totally different. He listens with attention and ruminates on what he hears and reads. Sometimes increasing and sometimes overturning his theories, he is always increasing his experience. He preserves the result but neglects the detail. The anecdotes that may happen to dwell in his mind are still without the accuracy of dates or names or places, and therefore cannot be produced in conversation.

Listening with attention, and ruminating on what he heard and read, Sir Joshua developed the habit of putting on paper some of his theories about life and art.[1] He had an inquiring mind; he was an amateur psychologist; he early accustomed himself to studying faces and penetrating to the personality behind the mask; he displayed particular interest in literature and literary men. It is therefore not surprising that he tried his hand at writing biographical sketches of a few friends. In his lifetime his reputation as a writer was derived from his *Discourses on Painting*, which he wrote for the students of the Royal Academy. Equally interesting—to some readers more interesting—are the character sketches of some of his friends, which he never published, and which are here brought together for the first time.

§ 4

In our day the personality of Sir Joshua has been misunderstood. He has been depicted as mercenary, pompous, self-centred. One author has gone so far as to describe him as a "sinuous climber and polished hypocrite".[2] He seems to be paying the penalty for having been over-praised in his lifetime. Not that he escaped adverse criticism in his own day. As Burke put it, "he had too much merit not to excite some jealousy." But those who attacked him were for the most part those who did not know him well, and surely such people are not the authorities to which we should turn. The composite picture of the man which derives from reputable sources is a remarkably flattering one.

Reference has already been made to the mock epitaph in

[1] Some of these notes, which were discovered among the Boswell Papers, are printed in Appendix III.

[2] Such a characterisation derives, I suspect, from the vitriolic comments of William Blake. For example: "I consider Reynolds's *Discourses* . . . as the simulation of the hypocrite who smiles particularly when he means to betray. His praise of Raphael is like the hysteric smile of revenge; his softness and candour the hidden trap and the poisoned feast."

Goldsmith's *Retaliation*, by far the pleasantest of the various epitaphs Goldsmith wrote. What is there emphasised is Sir Joshua's equable temper. Nowhere is this better revealed than in the verses written by his close friend Thomas Barnard, who later became Bishop of Killaloe.

> Dear knight of Plympton, teach me how
> To suffer, with unruffled brow
> And smile serene, like thine,
> The jest uncouth or truth severe;
> To such I'll turn my deafest ear
> And calmly drink my wine.
>
> Thou say'st not only skill is gained
> But genius too may be attained
> By studious imitation;
> Thy temper mild, thy genius fine
> I'll copy till I make them mine
> By constant application.

This is the picture of him which was shared by young and old, men and women. "Cherish Sir Joshua with your company, and enliven him by your conversation," wrote the learned Samuel Parr to Boswell late in 1791. "In taste, in judgment, in felicity of style and urbanity of manners, he is among the first of men, and there are qualities of a yet higher order which give him a place among the best of men."

He certainly inspired the affection of his friends. With his disciples it was something more like veneration. Young James Northcote, a sharp-tongued critic of men and manners, lived as a pupil with Sir Joshua for some four years. When he was about to depart, he wrote to his family: "I know him thoroughly, and all his faults, I am sure, and yet almost worship him." The word *worship* is a second cast; originally Northcote had written *adore*.

Mrs. Thrale is on record as not really liking Reynolds. "I always told Johnson," she wrote in *Thraliana*, "that they overrated that man's mental qualities. He replied, 'Everybody loves Reynolds except *you*.' The truth is, I felt that he hated *me*." He was, she thought, a bit too cool, a bit too lacking in human sympathy. Her pen-portrait of him is therefore useful to us as a corrective.

> Of Reynolds what good shall be said?—or what harm?
> His temper too frigid, his pencil too warm;
> A rage for sublimity ill understood,
> To seek still for the great, by forsaking the good;
> Yet all faults from his converse we sure must disclaim,
> As his temper 'tis peaceful, and pure as his fame.
> Nothing in it o'erflows, nothing ever is wanting;
> It nor chills like his kindness, nor glows like his painting.
> When Johnson by strength overpowers our mind,
> When Montagu dazzles, and Burke strikes us blind,
> To Reynolds for refuge well pleased we can run,
> Rejoice in his shadow, and shrink from the sun.

These lines, which the author herself wished she could have made more favourable, cannot be brushed aside as untrue. Northcote, we have just seen, realised that his master had faults, and we know from the conversations of his old age that the faults he noted were those pointed out by Mrs. Thrale. They are the faults which one would expect to find in a man of Sir Joshua's temperament. He was no Samuel Johnson. Johnson, deeply passionate by nature, loved a good hater. Sir Joshua often remarked that he hated nobody. As a corollary one might say that he was somewhat lacking in a capacity for love. In this connection the reasons he gave Boswell for never marrying are significant. When Malone (a bachelor) "strangely maintained that a man has the same fondness, as a lover, for a woman who has been for years his own as for the finest woman whom he has never possessed", Reynolds, after denying this, added "that something else very comfortable, very valuable, came in place of fondness when there had been possession; there was then affection, friendship. He said the reason why he would never marry was that every woman whom he had liked had grown indifferent to him, and he had been glad that he did not marry her".

That Sir Joshua had faults is only another way of saying that he was human. But to stress these faults is to alter the picture which has come down to us from many sources. On this point Burke's opinion as expressed to his friend Malone is authoritative. "He enjoyed every circumstance of his good fortune, and had no affectation on that subject. I do not know a fault or weakness of his that he did not convert into something that bordered on a virtue, instead of pushing to the confines of a vice."

This statement, made in a letter which Burke did not write for publication, takes us back to where we started, the obituary which was his official pronouncement. In it, as we have seen, Burke speaks of his friend as "a profound and penetrating philosopher", a man with "native humility, modesty, and candour", who possessed "talents of every kind . . . not meanly cultivated by letters". What such a person had to say about some of the distinguished contemporaries whom he knew intimately demands our attention. But before examining Sir Joshua's portraits one question must be disposed of. And this question leads us to James Boswell.

II

BOSWELL AND REYNOLDS

Not least among the many delightful surprises that came with the discovery of Boswell's archives was the material that makes up the greater part of this book. There had been no hint that these manuscripts ever existed. Nor was there any reason to suppose that materials of this sort would be among those that Boswell had in his possession. It has long been known that he carefully saved letters which he had received from his celebrated contemporaries. It was known that he systematically collected anything he could lay his hands upon which pertained to Dr. Johnson or to the Boswell family. What could not have been predicted was that his collection also included a batch of Sir Joshua's private papers.

How Boswell acquired these papers is still a mystery and will presumably never be known with certainty. All one can do is to hazard a guess, and the guess necessitates a review of the relations between the two men.

Reynolds and Boswell were first brought together by Goldsmith in 1769. By that time both were famous. Reynolds, President of the newly-founded Royal Academy, had just been knighted. Boswell, seventeen years younger and about to celebrate his twenty-ninth birthday, was revelling in the success of his first book. We are inclined to forget the extraordinary impact which his *Corsica* made, not only in England but on the Continent as well. His name was constantly in the newspapers; his book had already gone through three editions in England and three in Ireland, and had been translated into Dutch, French, German, and Italian.

It was not long before the two established a friendship which was to last uninterruptedly until Sir Joshua's death more than twenty years later. When Boswell was admitted to the English Bar, Reynolds attended the inauguration dinner; when Reynolds was invited to a formal dinner given by one of the London guilds, Boswell was his guest. Boswell took Reynolds to see criminals hanged and accompanied him when a private collection of paintings was to be viewed. Sir Joshua was one of the select few who passed judgment on Boswell's *Tour of the Hebrides* before it was published; Boswell was one of the distinguished guests who sat in the front row when Reynolds lectured at the Royal Academy. Boswell's journal has many entries recording the pleasant times they had together. "We drew close to the fire and took a cordial glass *tête-a-tête*, excluding the cold, which was intense. . . . I was fatigued by travelling in the mail coach in a cold, frosty night, and coming home from the City at four in the morning; but a warm bed and then Sir Joshua's revived me. . . . Dined at Sir Joshua's quietly, nobody there. . . . Much pleasantry at Sir Joshua's where the Gang went afterwards. Sat till about twelve over fine punch. . . . With Sir Joshua in his coach to Mr. Wilkes's at Kensington Gore, where we had an excellent entertainment. . . . Adjourned to Sir Joshua's and eat oysters and drank some punch very pleasantly."

Hitherto unpublished letters between the two, discovered among the Boswell Papers, give a fresh view of their friendship. The earliest of these is Boswell's copy of a gay letter he wrote to Reynolds at the time when Johnson was finishing his *Lives of the Poets*.

Edinburgh, 27 February 1781

DEAR SIR,

During the long intervals of my absence from London, I have often wished to have the pleasure of hearing from you; and when we last shook hands at parting, you said, "Write to me, and I'll answer you." Yet by some strange imbecility or distraction of mind, though I have many a time sat down to begin a letter to you, this (if I shall make it out) will be the first that I have ended. The truth is, that in this dull northern town I am not the same man that you see in the metropolis. I have not that jocund complacency, that eager gaiety, which you have frequently cherished. Allow me, dear Sir, to begin our correspondence with returning you my most sincere thanks for your goodness to me, which has increased every year since I was fortunate enough to be introduced to your acquaintance. To make this grateful acknowledgment is a real satisfaction.

I long much for more of our wonderful (*mirabilis*) friend Dr. Johnson's *Prefaces to the Poets*. The criticism and biography of those I have read delight me more and more.[1] What a pity it is that he loathes so much to write, and since that is the case, what a pity it is that there is not constantly with him such a recorder of his conversation as I am. I hope next month to be again in London and resume that office. But you must write to me by way of a cheering welcome. You must not delay. You must "answer me" as you said you would do. We have lost Beauclerk and Chamier since I was with you. These are sad losses. The first never can be repaired, though his acidity sometimes made me smart.[2]

[1] Four of the ten volumes of Johnson's *Prefaces, Biographical and Critical* had been published in 1779. The remaining six were about to be published.

[2] Both Topham Beauclerk (1739–1780) and the politician Anthony Chamier (1725–1780) were original members of the Club. Five years earlier Boswell wrote in his journal for 11 April: "At this time in London I was wearing out as my dress suit an old crimson suit embroidered with silver, made at Dublin in 1769. It was now old fashioned, though a good handsome dress. I said, 'I feel myself quite different in this suit from what I am in my frock' (meaning that I felt myself better). Said Beauclerk: 'So should I feel myself quite different, but I should not feel agreeably' (meaning that I was ridiculous). He has a fine malignity about him."

I saw at Chester a Miss Cunliffe, whom I liked exceedingly.[1] She was very amiable, and painted surprisingly well. She told me she had been obliged to you for allowing her to copy some of your pictures. But she would not be called by me a scholar of Sir Joshua's. I thought you would be very well pleased to be her master—"And teach my lovely scholar all I know."[2]

I hope when we meet I shall receive from you some valuable additions to my Boswelliana. I am, with great regard, dear Sir, your obliged and affectionate humble servant.

The most chatty of the new letters from Reynolds to Boswell was written a year and a half later. Boswell had for a long time been fighting an inward battle. His sense of duty told him that he should practise the law in Scotland; his inclination tempted him to settle in London as a barrister. Just as duty was apparently winning out, the following letter reached him, a letter which he endorsed: "Received 17 October 1782. Sir Joshua Reynolds: an agreeable letter of friendship."

[1] Daughter of Sir Ellis Cunliffe, Bart., M.P., and a leading citizen of Chester. In 1780 Boswell's friend Margaret Stuart wrote to him that when in Chester she had been particularly pleased with Miss Cunliffe's sense, spirit, and vivacity and with Miss Mary Cunliffe's beauty. Which of the two sisters was the painter is not known. Mary was the elder, Margaret Elizabeth the younger.

[2] What joy to wind along the cool retreat,
To stop, and gaze on Delia as I go!
To mingle sweet discourse with kisses sweet,
And teach my lovely scholar all I know!

JAMES HAMMOND'S *Elegy XIII.*

In 1784 Sir Joshua wrote: "If all those whom I have endeavoured to help forward by lending them pictures and telling them their faults should do me the honour of calling themselves my scholars, I should have the greatest school that ever painter had. If those young painters think that from such an intercourse they have a right to say they are my scholars, they are very welcome. I have no kind of objection to it."

London, 1 October 1782

DEAR BOSWELL,

I take it very kindly that you are so good as to write to me, though I have been so backward in answering your letters. If I felt the same reluctance in taking a pencil in my hand as I do a pen, I should be as bad a painter as I am a correspondent. Everybody has their taste. I love the correspondence of *viva voce* over a bottle with a great deal of noise and a great deal of nonsense.

Mr. Burke dined with me yesterday. He talked much of you and with great affection. He says you are the pleasantest man he ever saw and sincerely wishes you would come and live amongst us.[1] All your friends here, I believe, will subscribe to that wish. Suppose we send you a Round Robin, such as we sent to Dr. Johnson, to invite you. Will that be an inducement? I think I have many in my eye that would be eager to subscribe. What d'ye think of Lord Keppel and the franker of this letter?[2]

[1] Reynolds had quoted this opinion of Burke's in the letter he had just written to Langton. *See below*, p. 156.

[2] Augustus, first Viscount Keppel (1725–1786), now an admiral, had when a captain in 1749 taken Reynolds to the Mediterranean and thus made it possible for him to study in Italy. In 1779 he had been court-martialled on a charge that was found to be "malicious and ill-founded". When he was acquitted there were celebrations throughout the country. The "franker of this letter" was the Cornish politician Edward Eliot (1727–1804), a patron of Sir Joshua's. (Members of Parliament were accustomed to frank the letters of others as well as their own.) Eliot had delighted Boswell the year before by introducing him to the Cornish drink called *mahogany*, two parts gin and one part treacle. On 6 February 1784 Boswell, hearing that Eliot had been created Baron Eliot of Port Eliot, wrote to Reynolds: "But only why, oh why, did he not obtain the title of Baron *Mahogany*? Genealogists and heralds would have had curious work of it to explain and illustrate that title."

My dear Sir, I had wrote thus far above a week since, but having never spent an evening at home, neglected finishing it. I find by the papers that you have lost your father, for which I sincerely condole with you, but I hope this accident will not remove at a further distance the hope of seeing you in London.

I am, dear Sir,

Yours most affectionately,

J. REYNOLDS

The flattering remarks of Burke, and the allusion to "all your friends", to say nothing of "the correspondence of *viva voce* over a bottle", would naturally revive in Boswell all his desires to establish himself in London. No letter from Reynolds better reveals the place which Boswell had won for himself in the affections of Sir Joshua's circle. Years later Mary Palmer told the artist Farington that she had been annoyed by Boswell's company—he was disposed to come too often and stay too late—but that her uncle was never tired of seeing him. This letter corroborates the statement.

Sir Joshua played a part second only to Malone in encouraging Boswell to get on with the writing of the *Life of Johnson*. And Boswell, who had honoured Malone in his first Johnsonian book, the *Tour to the Hebrides*, dedicated the *Life* to Reynolds. The book was published in May, 1791, and that summer Boswell was in Scotland. His subsequent relations with Reynolds are best summed up in his copy of an unpublished letter in the Boswell Papers. It was written to Thomas Barnard, Bishop of Killaloe, in the middle of February, 1792, a week before Sir Joshua died.

When I came to town in October, I found him in great apprehension of losing the sight of his other eye; on which account he had taken a number of medicines and lived very low, so that he was relaxed and dejected. He by Dr. Warren's advice made some efforts to rouse his constitution, but he soon sunk again, and by degrees became so ill as to be confined to his room, and for more than a month he has kept his bed. The physicians were long entirely in the dark as to his case. Dr. Warren said to me that it was a dissolution of his frame occasioned by some disorder which could not be discerned. A few days ago they thought they had discovered it to be a diseased liver, and they are now treating him accordingly, but have no hope of his recovery. He does not wish to see his friends, takes laudanum, and dozes in "tranquil despondency", as Burke expressed it. His death will be an irreparable loss to the Academy and to his numerous friends. The thought of it hangs heavy upon my mind.

In the "official" biography Malone says that Reynolds "was wholly unable to explain to his physicians the nature or seat of his disorder". His friends thought that his illness was imaginary; "at length (but not till about a fortnight before his death) the seat of his disorder was found to be in his liver, of which the inordinate growth, as it afterwards appeared, had incommoded all the functions of life; and of this disease, which he bore with the greatest fortitude and patience, he died after a confinement of near three months . . . on Thursday evening, Feb. 23, 1792."

Six months later Boswell again wrote to the Bishop of Killaloe:

Everything concerning the loss of our ever-to-be-lamented Sir Joshua Reynolds has long ago reached your Lordship. I heartily wish that in one respect he had been such as *we* are.[1]

[1] In the preceding letter to the Bishop, Boswell had written: "I am very sorry that he did not imbibe Christian piety from Johnson. No clergyman attends him; no holy rites console his languishing hours. I heartily wish that your Lordship were here."

But we must make allowance and hope the best. Cosway[1] says he will be *retarded* in his spiritual progress. The blank which he makes in the circle in which I have long moved is sad indeed. Malone is editing his discourses and some other writings concerning his art. The world will have it that I am to be his biographer. I did begin last winter to collect some particulars of his early life from him. Tomorrow I am to set out on a jaunt into Devonshire and Cornwall and, I doubt not, shall pick up a variety of materials for his history. But whether I shall attempt what as yet seems not quite well suited to me I know not. Sir Joshua was indeed a man of pleasing and various conversation, but he had not those prominent features which can be seized like Johnson's. Our friends of the Royal Academy urge me to the task by telling me that I may make a very good book of the late President's life, interwoven with the history of the arts during his time, and they will contribute all their lights.

This would seem to be the first reference by Boswell to his projected *Life of Reynolds*. A few months earlier Bishop Percy had told Mrs. Piozzi that Boswell was to undertake the task. "Let us be careful of our health, my Lord," she replied, "or he will write *our* lives too." Among the Boswell Papers is Boswell's copy of an unpublished letter to his friend Andrew Erskine, dated 6 March 1793. Malone, he writes, is editing the literary works of

that most ingenious and amiable man—I had almost used the lady's word *charming*. The last year of his life, I began to take

[1] Richard Cosway (1740–1821), the painter, who had been elected a Royal Academician in 1771.

notes from him of his early years and also indeed of other periods of his progress to that pinnacle of excellence which he reached; and when I was in Devonshire and Cornwall last autumn I got several anecdotes concerning him. But I doubt much whether I could write a life of him. Lord Macartney indeed suggested to me that if I pleased I might make a wonderful book by giving a *catalogue raisonné* of all those whose portraits he painted and all those whom he should have painted, and added that he would furnish me with many materials.

The letter just quoted contains the second reference to notes of a biographical sort which Boswell wrote shortly before Sir Joshua's death. Luckily some of these (perhaps all that were made) are preserved in the Boswell Papers and show the great biographer at work. They are jotted down on a letter, written on a Tuesday, which Boswell had just received from his brother David, reminding him that he and his four children were expected at David's for a turkey dinner on 2 January 1792 and asking whether David's family was to dine with Boswell on Christmas Day. Halfway through the biographical notes is the parenthetical remark "said he smiling, 20 December 1791", an indication that David's note was written on Tuesday, 20 December, received that day by Boswell as he was on his way to call on Reynolds, and offered the most convenient bit of blank paper to Boswell when he wished to record what the dying Sir Joshua was telling him of his early life.

Sir Joshua Reynolds. His father was very fond of drawings (query if he drew himself), and loved to encourage his children in drawing. His two eldest sisters did little things (query what), and he copied them. He used to copy all the

Sir J. R. His Father was very fond of
drawings, & loved to encourage his children in
drawing. His two elder sisters did little things (Q what)
& he copied them. He used to copy all the frontispieces
& plates in Books particularly those in Plutarch's Lives
But his great fund of imitation was Jacob Catts's Book
which his Grandmother a Dutchwoman had brought over
At eight years old he read eagerly [illegible] Perspective
which taught him it so well, he has never studied any book
on it since. He drew the school at Plympton which is founded
on granite pillars (Q) & he did it so well that his Father
said. Now this exemplifies what the Author says in his
Preface that by observing these rules a man may
do wonders; for this is wonderful. He then
began to try likenesses of relations & friends — rubbed
them out & did them again. When he read
Richardson's Principles of Painting he was struck
with admiration of the Art — thought it beyond
all others — thought Raphael beyond Pope &
all eminent persons — And indeed (said he smiling 20 Decr. 1791)
I have indulged that notion all along. He did not employ
himself much in Landscape. He has done one of Richmond not very well (Q where) And one of which
Lord [illegible] has. But he observed that he wished only
for as much of it as to form a background for a Picture
[illegible] said he contrived [illegible] & every historical
painter must be able to paint both portrait and
Landscape. He had thought too mechanical [illegible]
either as to painting; for he held there was
no particular natural genius & that any child might be
taught to do a portrait some better, some worse no doubt. He

FIRST PAGE OF BOSWELL'S NOTES
FOR A BIOGRAPHY OF REYNOLDS

"The last year of his life I began to take notes from him of his early years and also indeed of other periods of his progress to that pinnacle of excellence which he reached."—Boswell

frontispieces and plates in books, particularly those in Plutarch's *Lives*. But his great fund of imitation was Jacob Cats's Book [of Emblems] which his grandmother, a Dutchwoman,[1] had brought over. At eight years old he read eagerly [*The Jesuit*]'*s Perspective*, which taught him it so well, he has never studied any book on it since. He drew the school at Plympton, which is founded on granite pillars (query), and he did it so well that his father said, "Now this exemplifies what the author says in his preface, that by observing these rules a man may do wonders; for this is wonderful." He then began to try likenesses of relations and friends—rubbed them out and did them again. When he read Richardson's *Principles of Painting*, he was struck with admiration of the art—thought it beyond all others—thought Raphael beyond Pope and all eminent persons—"and indeed" (said he smiling, 20 December 1791) "I have indulged that notion all along". He did not employ himself much in landscape. He has done one of Richmond not very well (query where) and one of [Plymouth Sound] which [Lord Eliot] has.[2] But he observed that he wished only for as much of it as to form a background for a picture. "*Majus*", said he, "*continet minus*; and every historical painter

[1] An error which is found in most of the biographies of Reynolds. His paternal grandmother was Mary Ainsworth. "Her father, Henry Ainsworth, lived at Exeter and carried on a large trade with the Low Countries, having a branch house of business in Antwerp, owning ships as well as dealing in merchandise."

[2] The landscape of Richmond was in Sir Joshua's house when Boswell wrote his notes. It remained in the family until 1821, when it was sold at auction to Samuel Rogers. The other landscape mentioned is probably that which was painted in 1748 and has always been at Port Eliot.

must be able to paint both portrait and landscape." He had, I thought, too mechanical a notion as to painting; for he held there was no particular natural genius, and that any child not defective in organs might be taught to do a portrait—some better, some worse, no doubt.

He entered to paint with Mr. Hudson in [1740]. While with him, Cox the auctioneer was selling Lord Oxford's pictures in Covent Garden. The room was much crowded. Pope came in. Immediately it was mentioned he was there, a lane was made for him to walk through. Everyone in the front rows by a kind of enthusiastic impulse shook hands with him. Reynolds did like the rest and was very happy in having that opportunity.[1] Pope was seldom seen in public, so it was a great sight to see him. He got within the rails at the head of the room. Sir Joshua said he had an extraordinary face, not an everyday countenance—a pallid, studious look; not merely a sharp, keen countenance, but something grand, like Cicero's. It was like what Petronius Arbiter says, [*grandiaque indomiti Ciceronis verba*].[2] He said there was an appearance about his

[1] Our knowledge of this well-known meeting has hitherto been based on Northcote's account, but Boswell's version adds specific information. If young Reynolds saw Pope at the sale of Oxford's pictures, the incident can be dated between 8 and 13 March 1742, two years before Pope's death. Oxford had been one of Pope's closest friends, and Cock (not Cox) was the leading auctioneer of the day. In 1744 he was immortalised in Fielding's *Joseph Andrews*: "Mr. Cock . . . appeared aloft in his pulpit, trumpeting forth the praises of a china basin and with astonishment wondering that 'nobody bids more for that fine, that superb—'."

[2] "And lofty words of undaunted Cicero." This phrase, from the fifth section of the *Satyricon*, was kindly suggested by Professor C. W. Mendell.

mouth which is found only in [the] deformed, and from which he could have known him to be deformed.[1]

Even in his rough notes Boswell vitalises his subject. At least some of Sir Joshua's remarks are quoted as direct discourse, and the word *smiling*, an afterthought tucked in above the line, makes all the difference between dry facts and a living picture.

Boswell died in the spring of 1795, but well before his death he had abandoned his scheme of writing this life. One sentence in an obituary of Boswell reads: "It was Boswell's intention to have given a biographical account of Sir Joshua, but as the domestic particulars of that artist were but few and as Boswell did not profess to know much of painting, he relinquished the idea very properly, considering it the province of a painter to raise a professional monument to the British Apelles." This would seem to be borne out by the comments Boswell makes in the two letters quoted above, but just before he died he told Farington that though he "had serious intentions" of writing this life, he was conscious that he might offend Mary Palmer, now Lady Inchiquin, since he believed Reynolds to have been to blame in a quarrel which he had had with the Academy at the end of his life.

Though he never pushed the scheme, we now know definitely that he was collecting materials. It is therefore reasonable to suppose that the Reynolds papers which turned up in Malahide Castle were acquired with a view to their use in a biography. Why he took these particular papers, and only these, it would, in Johnson's phrase, be fruitless to inquire. The bulk of Sir Joshua's manuscripts were retained by Mary Palmer, and most of them are now in the Royal Academy.

It is a pity that Boswell did not write at least a short life of Reynolds. Sir Joshua's conversation, to be sure, lacked the force of Johnson's—did not "teem with point". But Boswell could have done much which would illustrate the remark he made in his

[1] Pope, who suffered from tuberculosis of the vertebral column, was a hunchback. He was described by Voltaire as "protuberant before and behind".

journal: "Sir Joshua completes a saying. He is like a jeweller. You bring him a diamond; he cuts it, and makes it much more brilliant." Boswell could have displayed Sir Joshua's good humour and method of bringing out the best in other people. He could have given us vivid sketches of those *noctes coenaeque Deum* which gave him such delight. And he could have treated his subject with much the same reverence that he accorded Paoli and Johnson. As late as 1785, after Reynolds had given him a lecture on morality, Boswell wrote: "I am very lucky in my intimacy with this eminent man."

III

GOLDSMITH AND REYNOLDS

§ 1

In 1845 B. R. Haydon the painter journeyed to Plymouth to call upon the "last relic left of the Johnsonian-Burkeian period." She was Theophila Palmer Gwatkin, sister of Mary Palmer and niece of Sir Joshua. Haydon "found on a sofa, leaning on pillows, a venerable aged lady, holding an ear-trumpet like Sir Joshua, showing in her face great remains of regular beauty. . . ". When she rose, "her figure was fine and elastic, upright as a dart, with nothing of decrepitude; certainly extraordinary for a woman in her eighty-ninth year". Soon she was chatting animatedly about events which had taken place seventy-five years earlier, when as "quite a little girl" she had gone to London to live with her uncle. Of all the famous men whom she met there, the most delightful, she thought, was Goldsmith. Johnson's bluntness terrified her, but she was able to talk to Goldsmith as to a contemporary, and his behaviour in society was the sort which would naturally please a child. She remembered him and Garrick keeping "an immense party laughing till they shrieked. Garrick sat on Goldsmith's knee; a table-cloth was pinned under Garrick's chin and brought behind Goldsmith, hiding both their figures. Garrick then spoke, in his finest style, Hamlet's speech on his father's ghost. Goldsmith put out his hands on each side of the cloth and made burlesque action, tapping his heart and putting his hand to Garrick's head and nose, all at the wrong time."

This is hardly the picture we should expect of a man who had written of polite learning in Europe (where, be it noted, he had attacked Garrick), or of the evils of the penal code or the acts of enclosure. It is not what we should expect of a highly celebrated author in the days when gentlemen wore wigs and coloured silk coats, satin breeches and silk stockings. Nevertheless the incident which had made such an impression on Offy Palmer is thoroughly characteristic of Oliver Goldsmith.

Goldsmith's personal appearance is familiar to us through Sir Joshua's well-known portrait, which, a contemporary reported to Smollett, resembled Goldsmith greatly. Frances Reynolds admitted that it was a good likeness, although a flattering one. Mary Horneck, whom Goldsmith called "the Jessamy bride", thought it conveyed "a good idea of his face; it was painted as a fine poetical head for the admiration of posterity, but as it is divested of his wig and with the shirt collar open, it was not the man as seen in daily life". Her qualification is an important one. Almost without exception Reynolds painted his sitters as they were seen in daily life—that is, as they appeared at an assembly, complete with all their finery and in a dignified pose. Why should he have departed from his usual practice when painting Goldsmith? Assuredly this was no accident. Robert Selby, who was sixteen when Goldsmith lived in the Selbys' house, later said that when at home the poet usually "wore his shirt collar open in the manner represented in the portrait by Sir Joshua". Reynolds was painting the man he saw. He might have painted him proudly arrayed in his bloom-coloured coat. Instead, by portraying him without his wig and in informal dress he is saying, as clearly as can be said in painting, that Goldsmith was essentially a simple person, unpretentious and unaffected. That is the impression which Goldsmith made on young Northcote, who, after meeting him for the first time, wrote to his brother: "You would very much like him, he has so much good nature and no conceit or affectation."

No one knew Goldsmith better than Sir Joshua. The two had first met, it seems, in 1762. At that time Reynolds was well established as the leading portrait-painter of the day, and Goldsmith was already recognised as the author of *An Enquiry into the Present State of Polite Learning*, *The Bee*, and *The Citizen of the World*. Early in 1762 he had been singled out by a journalist as a man "surpassed by few of his contemporaries with regard to the matter which his

OLIVER GOLDSMITH, BY REYNOLDS

"Miss Reynolds said of this portrait that it was a very great likeness of the Doctor, but the most flattered picture she ever knew her brother to have painted."—NORTHCOTE

writings contain", and "superior to most of them in style, having happily found out the secret to unite elevation with ease, a perfection in language which few writers of our nation have attained to, as most of those who aim at sublimity swell their expressions with fustian and bombast, whilst those who affect ease degenerate into familiarity and flatness".

Such a notice, we are told by Mrs. Thrale, would result in Reynolds seeking out the author and forming an acquaintance with him. Certainly they had established a friendship by 1764 and for the last ten years of Goldsmith's life were constantly together. Both of course were charter members of the Club, but saw much more of each other elsewhere. "Sir Joshua and Goldsmith", wrote Beauclerk, "have got into such a round of pleasures that they have no time [for the Club]." They dined and supped together; they were seen at Vauxhall or the theatre together; they played draughts together; they "unbosomed their minds freely to each other". Sir Joshua interceded with Garrick on Goldsmith's behalf when *The Good Natured-Man* was written. He arranged to have Goldsmith appointed Historian of the Royal Academy. He dedicated to Goldsmith the engraving of one of his studies.

Goldsmith on his part publicly called attention to their friendship when in 1770 he dedicated to Reynolds *The Deserted Village*. The first paragraph illustrates how effectively Goldsmith could write simple English without degenerating "into familiarity and flatness". "I can have no expectations, in an address of this kind, either to add to your reputation, or to establish my own. You can gain nothing from my admiration, as I am ignorant of that art in which you are said to excel: and I may lose much by the severity of your judgment, as few have a juster taste in poetry than you. Setting interest therefore aside, to which I never paid much attention, I must be indulged at present in following my affections. The only dedication I ever made was to my brother, because I loved him better than most other men. He is since dead. Permit me to inscribe this poem to you."

Perhaps the best index to their friendship is to be found in the charming letter Goldsmith wrote to Reynolds from the Continent.

It begins with, for him, the rather unusual "My dear Friend," and contains such passages as: "You see by the top of this letter that we are at Paris, and (as I have often heard you say) we have brought our own amusement with us, for the ladies do not seem to be very fond of what we have yet seen. . . . One of our chief amusements here is scolding at every thing we meet with and praising every thing and every person we left at home. You may judge therefore whether your name is not frequently bandied at table among us. To tell you the truth, I never thought I could regret your absence so much as our various mortifications on the road have often taught me to do. I could tell you of disasters and adventures without number, of our lying in barns, and of my being half poisoned with a dish of green peas, of our quarrelling with postillions and being cheated by landladies, but I reserve all this for an happy hour which I expect to share with you upon my return. . . . For Godsake the night you receive this take your pen in your hand and tell me some thing about yourself and myself, if you know of anything that has happened. . . . Is there any thing I can do for you at Paris? I wish you would tell me. The whole of my own purchases here is one silk coat, which I have put on, and which makes me look like a fool. But no more of that. . . . I have one thing only more to say, and of that I think every hour in the day—namely, that I am your most sincere and most affectionate friend."

For a hostile view of the relations between the two men we must again turn to the caustic pen of Mrs. Thrale. Sir Joshua's thoughts, she wrote three years after Goldsmith's death, "are tending how to propagate letters written in his praise, how to make himself respected as a Doctor at Oxford, and how to disseminate his praise for himself, now Goldsmith is gone who used to do it for him. *He* was while he lived the person Sir Joshua seemed to have most friendship for; he lent him money, loved his company, and a *little* lamented his death. Truth is, Doctor Goldsmith loved him in return, a favour he paid to but few. We must remember, however, that Reynolds did not stand in his way, but enjoyed the bloom of a reputation perfectly consistent with his own."

It is unnecessary to point out that her words are loaded. But in view of her bias Mrs. Thrale's testimony is particularly valuable. Even she was witness to the close bond that united the two men.

§ 2

When Goldsmith died in April, 1774, "epigrams, epitaphs, and monodies to his memory were without end." Anecdotes illustrating his eccentricities appeared in the magazines and newspapers. His name and his fame were the principal topics of conversation. One day at Sir Joshua's table his weaknesses as a writer were being discussed by the company. The discussion ended abruptly when Johnson rose "with great dignity, looked them full in the face, and exclaimed, 'If nobody was suffered to abuse poor Goldy but those who could write as well, he would have few censors' ".

Percy, not yet a bishop, was by agreement to write the official biography. When Boswell called on him a year after Goldsmith's death, Percy "read to me anecdotes of Goldsmith, taken from his own mouth and confirmed by his brother Maurice Goldsmith, a cabinet-maker, who came over from Ireland on his death thinking to get something, when alas! poor Goldy was drowned in debt. He also showed me a bunch of papers of Goldsmith's which he had got from him in a present. They seemed to be just a handful of what was lying on his table or in his bureau: letters, notes, scraps of all kinds. Percy had also bits cut out of newspapers about him; in short, many materials for a life of him which he intended to write." Ten days later Percy's intention of writing the life was mentioned in Johnson's presence, and Johnson "expressed his approbation strongly".

The following year Nollekens was at work on the bust of Goldsmith which was placed in Westminster Abbey. In May Johnson sent his epitaph on Goldsmith to Sir Joshua, and soon after that at Sir Joshua's house the Round Robin concerning that epitaph was written to Johnson. Percy was still nominally the biographer and planned to prefix what he wrote to an edition of Goldsmith's poems, the proceeds of which were to go to the poet's brother Maurice. From Ireland in July Maurice sent letters and anecdotes to Percy as materials for the biography. "I can assure you, Sir," he writes (and the original spelling is here retained), "I have gon several Miles to Collect them, and as my Circumstances at present are not verry Affluent a small assistance wod be gratefully accepted, shd. any accrue from these papers, wich, with what my good Friend Sr. Josshua Reynolds and Mr. Garrick promisd to supply, will not be deemd I hope unworthy of yr publication, which you and Sir Josshua told me you wod get affected." This indicates that Reynolds had not only promised to help secure a publisher for the projected edition; he and Garrick, if Maurice's grammar is to be trusted, had agreed to contribute materials for the biography itself.

So far matters seem clear enough. From this point the story becomes foggy. Percy, presumably late in 1776, relinquished his task to Johnson, who not only received the papers and information already collected, but was in touch with the Goldsmith family and had enlisted the aid of Malone in gathering additional facts. Years later Malone spoke of Johnson's assignment as though it was to have appeared in the impressive edition of the English poets for which he was beginning to write prefaces. Certainly the original idea, as has already been said, was that it should be a separate publication. In any case Johnson did not do the job, and when he died Percy once more agreed to take the responsibility. In June, 1785, Reynolds wrote to Percy, again promising to help Maurice. Thereafter history is silent as to his share in the project. When Reynolds died in 1792, the biography had not yet been written.

Meanwhile, as we now know, Reynolds himself had drafted a memoir of his friend, which eventually found its way into Boswell's hands. How Boswell acquired it, or when, or why, is not known. At some time before the end of 1786 Boswell possessed an unfinished letter which Goldsmith had written to Reynolds from the Continent. He endorsed it "Original letter of Dr. Goldsmith to Sir Joshua Reynolds, who gave it to me", and presented it to Malone, who sent it on to Percy in December, 1786. Surely Boswell would have turned over the memoir at the same time, if it had been in his possession. In all probability it did not come into Boswell's hands until Sir Joshua lay on his death-bed.

The questions which the memoir immediately raises are at what time and for what purpose it was written. The first of these can be answered with some confidence. Sir Joshua's own note near the end of his account informs us that Nollekens was then at work on the monument which was placed in Westminster Abbey. Nollekens seems to have begun his task not long before the Round Robin was written and to have completed it soon after. In other words, it is apparent that Sir Joshua was writing the memoir in 1776, two years after Goldsmith's death. And it was in July, 1776, that Maurice Goldsmith referred to "papers" which Sir Joshua had promised to supply for the biography. The evidence is disappointingly slight. It may be, however, that Sir Joshua's memoir was to be printed with Percy's biography, or possibly incorporated in it. Percy's dilatory behaviour would account for the fact that Sir Joshua never completed his task.

§ 3

To some readers, no doubt, the memoir will seem surprisingly dispassionate, considering the intimacy that had existed between the two. Like his master Johnson, Sir Joshua felt himself bound to tell the truth, and if not the whole truth, nothing but the truth. And like Johnson he guarded against burying his subject in a mass of anecdotes.

Had he wished, Reynolds could have preserved many stories which would throw light on Goldsmith's character. He told Northcote, for example, that Goldsmith "was often obliged to supplicate a friend for the loan of ten pounds for his immediate relief; yet, if by accident a distressed petitioner told him a piteous tale—nay, if a subscription for any folly was proposed to him—he without any thought of his own poverty would with an air of generosity freely bestow on the person who solicited for it the very loan he had himself but just before obtained."

To offset the charges that Goldsmith was unsuccessful in contests of wit he might have included the anecdote which he recounted to Boswell. Goldsmith, sitting with Johnson and Reynolds, said he thought he could write a good fable, "mentioned the simplicity which that kind of composition requires, and observed that, in most fables, the animals introduced seldom talk in character. 'For instance (said he), the fable of the little fishes who saw birds fly over their heads and, envying them, petitioned Jupiter to be changed into birds. The skill (continued he) consists in making them talk like little fishes.' While he indulged himself in this fanciful reverie, he observed Johnson shaking his sides and laughing. Upon which he smartly proceeded, 'Why, Dr. Johnson, this is not so easy as you seem to think; for if you were to make little fishes talk, they would talk like WHALES.' "

A number of the stories which Reynolds used to tell about Goldsmith were repeated years later by Mrs. Gwyn, the former Mary Horneck. One wonders how much these stories had changed through the years. All that we can say is that she, who knew Goldsmith intimately and was devoted to him, is reported as telling them on Sir Joshua's authority. One concerns Goldsmith's early days in London, when he was practising as a doctor of medicine. The fashionable doctor was expected to appear in a velvet coat. Goldsmith conformed by buying a second-hand coat which had a conspicuous patch on the left breast. Wishing "to conceal what is considered too obvious a symptom of poverty, he was accustomed to place his hat over the patch, and retain it there carefully during the visit." This is obviously the same story as that related by Cornelia Knight in her autobiography. According to her version the coat had been a nobleman's and "there was visible on the breast a mark showing where a star[1] had been".

Sir Joshua told Mrs. Gwyn that he (or perhaps a friend) called on Goldsmith while he was writing *The Traveller* and found the poet

[1] Emblem of one of the Orders of Knighthood.

not pacing the floor or tearing his hair but teaching his dog to beg. Before him on the desk was the couplet he had just written, scornfully applied to the degenerate Italians:

> By sports like these are all their cares beguiled,
> The sports of children satisfy the child.

The appropriateness of the lines was pointed out to the poet, who laughingly admitted that his own behaviour had suggested the idea.

Soon after the Club was founded, Goldsmith was persuaded by some of his friends, Reynolds among them, to take up once more the practice of medicine in order to add to his income. A Mrs. Sidebotham, one of his acquaintances, summoned Dr. Goldsmith, who wrote out a prescription for her which was so unorthodox that the apothecary felt obliged to argue the matter with the doctor. Finally they agreed to let the lady decide which of the two she would follow. When she sided with the apothecary "Goldsmith quitted the house highly indignant, declaring to Sir Joshua he would leave off prescribing for friends. 'Do so, my dear Doctor,' replied Topham Beauclerk when he heard the story and afterwards jested with him on the subject; 'whenever you undertake to kill, let it be only your enemies.' "

Still another anecdote Mrs. Gwyn told as coming from Reynolds. Goldsmith, always in financial distress, was persuaded to buy an expensive costume to wear to a masquerade. After the party Reynolds called on him and discovered him "in something of a reverie, yet deliberately walking round the room and kicking a bundle before him in the manner of a football". The bundle, of course, was the costume. Goldsmith, regretting his folly in having bought it, "was determined in his own phrase, 'to have the value out of it in exercise.' "

These anecdotes, and many others which Reynolds might have recorded, find no place in the memoir. Anecdotal biography was beginning to be popular in the eighteenth century, but it was a kind of writing to which Sir Joshua was opposed in principle. Like Johnson he believed that the artist should not number the streaks of the tulip but should remark general properties and large appearances.

"I am very ready to allow," he told students of art, "that some circumstances of minuteness and particularity frequently tend to give an air of truth to a piece and to interest the spectator in an extraordinary manner. Such circumstances therefore cannot wholly be rejected. . . . However, the usual and most dangerous error is on the side of minuteness; and therefore I think caution most necessary where most have failed. The general idea constitutes real excellence."

Except for the delightful illustration of Goldsmith's ineptness in telling a story, Sir Joshua's memoir is devoid of anecdote. The manuscript, to be sure, includes one, but it is difficult to see how the author would have fitted it into the finished work.

> Mr. Ridge, a relation of Doctor Goldsmith, told me that the Doctor's father with great difficulty furnished him with forty pounds, with which he was to go to London and enter in the Temple; that the Doctor, passing through Dublin, went into Lucas's coffee-house, where he lost the forty pounds, sold his horse, and lost that money likewise. He then sold his boots, which sum served to defray his expenses back to his father's house.

Mr. Ridge is presumably the Irish barrister mentioned in *Retaliation*, but there is no evidence that he was one of Goldsmith's relatives. The story seems to combine two questionable tales later told by a sister. It sounds apocryphal. That Sir Joshua thought it worth recording, however, indicates that he considered it characteristic and not improbable.

§ 4

The Goldsmith that most people know is the Goldsmith who appears in the *Life of Johnson*, and Goldsmith's biographers have felt it necessary to spend much time depreciating and contradicting

Boswell in an effort to give a more balanced and more sympathetic account of their subject. In justice to Boswell we should remember that in the book he was writing Goldsmith inevitably played the part of Dr. Minor to Johnson's Dr. Major. Boswell devotes a mere three paragraphs to a sketch of Goldsmith. There he brings out his awkwardness in society, his envious disposition, his carelessness of speech, his lack of system—traits which all who knew the man noticed. There too, however, he brings out Goldsmith's generosity and declares that the reports of his being a fool in conversation have been greatly exaggerated. And with Boswell's detractors in mind there is irony in the fact that Goldsmith's wit is nowhere better shown than in the *Life of Johnson*.

True enough, Boswell did not have for him the respect that he had for Johnson or Paoli or Burke or Reynolds. A somewhat patronising tone is noted in his references to "honest Goldsmith". But analysis will show that it is not what Boswell himself says which creates the admittedly biased picture. His camera was trained on Johnson. He depicts Goldsmith in "vain competition" with Johnson, and most of the harsh judgments of Goldsmith are uttered by Johnson. Hence the total impression of the man one gets in the *Life* is hardly a flattering one. Among those who objected to it in Boswell's lifetime were Burke and Lord Charlemont, Steevens and Percy, Wilkes and Malone. Malone, for example, wrote to Percy in 1807: "I always made battle against Boswell's representation . . . in the *Life of Johnson*, and often expressed to him my opinion that he rated Goldsmith much too low."

That Sir Joshua agreed with Malone has long been known. Apparently he too argued the matter with Boswell, who, faithful chronicler that he was, recorded the disagreement in a footnote to the *Life*: "Sir Joshua Reynolds mentioned to me that he frequently heard Goldsmith talk warmly of the pleasure of being liked and observe how hard it would be if literary excellence should preclude a man from that satisfaction, which he perceived it often did, from the envy which attended it; and therefore Sir Joshua was convinced that he was intentionally more absurd, in order to lessen himself in social intercourse, trusting that his character would be sufficiently supported by his works. If it indeed was his intention to appear absurd in company, he was often very successful. But with due deference to Sir Joshua's ingenuity, I think the conjecture too refined."

Boswell's note, of course, was written long after Sir Joshua's memoir. It represents a highly condensed version of what Boswell understood Sir Joshua's opinion to be. What Sir Joshua's opinion actually was we are now in a position to know. The memoir here first printed is his carefully considered statement, written for publication and at length. In it he accounts in part for Goldsmith's awkwardness in company by reminding us that he "came late into the great world", that with the publication of *The Traveller* in 1764 Goldsmith, like a later poet who wrote of his travels, awoke to find himself famous. But Reynolds also develops the thesis which he advanced to Boswell. He believed that *at times* Goldsmith deliberately behaved as he did because of his innate honesty and hatred of all that was pompous. In his writings Goldsmith is prone to attack the over-solemn, and often displays his fondness for what in one place he calls "agreeable trifling". His behaviour in society, according to Reynolds, was of a piece with this.

Furthermore, Sir Joshua maintained, this intentional absurdity was commonly misunderstood. As an illustration he cited the Malagrida story, though unfortunately he does no more than cite it. An example which he might have used is the anecdote which Boswell, speaking of Goldsmith's envious nature, was to mention in passing: "When accompanying two beautiful young ladies with their mother on a tour in France, he was seriously angry that more attention was paid to them than to him." One of the beautiful ladies, Mrs. Gwyn, gave her version of the story in later years, saying that when she and her sister had attracted the attention of some French officers, "Goldsmith seemed amused; but at length, assuming something of severity of countenance, which was a peculiarity of his humour often displayed when most disposed to be jocular, turned off, uttering something to the effect of what is commonly stated, that elsewhere he would also have his admirers." Significantly Mrs. Gwyn added: "This was said in mere playfulness, and I was shocked many years afterwards to see it adduced in print as a proof of his envious disposition."

But Reynolds admits that, though Goldsmith often deliberately played the clown, he was quite as often, to use Boswell's term, an *étourdi*. The specific example which he gives of this, surely a passage that will henceforth live in literature, is Goldsmith's story of the cobbler. And this story, if placed next to a passage in the *Vicar*, nicely illustrates the central problem confronting Goldsmith's biographer. When telling the story of the cobbler, Goldsmith breaks all the rules of story-telling, commencing with the promise that what he is about to tell will be a good story and a funny one. Now note what he has Mrs. Primrose say in the *Vicar*: "I'll tell you a good story about that, that will make you split your sides with laughing." No character in the *Vicar* is more heavily satirised than Mrs. Primrose. Can we believe that the author himself could be guilty of the same blunders?

The answer to that question must be in the affirmative. Reynolds tells us that Goldsmith would begin speaking before he had thought out what he wanted to say. Apparently he would plunge in, find to his chagrin that he was being foolish, and yet be incapable of extricating himself. No doubt it would be after unhappily floundering in this way that he would show himself, in Johnson's phrase, "irascible as a hornet"—would be humiliated, angry at himself, envious of those who could talk well. Then, when he began to write, the follies he himself had committed would serve as the materials on which his gentle satire played.[1]

Presumably Reynolds would accept everything that Boswell said of Goldsmith as true. What he would object to would be one-

[1] Professor Pottle suggests as analogous the sort of character found in many of Dostoevski's tales, who when by himself can see absurdity better than most of those who shine in society, but when in company is perversely absurd, a part of his mind all the time angrily aware of his folly. I take this opportunity of acknowledging my indebtedness to Professor Pottle, who has sternly forced me to re-examine the evidence on which this section is based, and whose interpretation I have in large measure adopted as my own.

sidedness and over-simplification. In his memoir of Johnson he wrote: "A short book containing an account of all the peculiarities or absurdities of a man would leave on the reader's mind an impression of an absurd character."[1] And at the beginning of his sketch of Goldsmith he points out that so unusually complex a person presents a challenge to a biographer. He accepted that challenge, indicated some of the complexities, and revealed his own powers of discrimination in accounting for them.

The importance of Sir Joshua's memoir should be obvious. He has reconciled seeming contradictions and made it possible for us to fit into his picture the conflicting stories that have come down to us from other sources. It is by no means a honeysuckle sketch. It is an essay on a man in whom we find "chaos of thought and passion, all confused". It is a posthumous portrait which has captured elements that make the man seem to come to life. Goldsmith was the subject of many contemporary biographical sketches. In authenticity, in profundity, none can compete with Sir Joshua's.

§ 5

The first printing of so important a manuscript presents problems. The reading public will naturally wish to know what Sir Joshua thought of Goldsmith; the specialist will want to have before him everything which Sir Joshua wrote on the subject. There would be no problem if all that we had was a finished account, ready for the printer. But in fact, what we have is a group of preliminary notes, a rough draft of the central part of the essay, and a revised and expanded version which lacks a beginning and an ending. The revised version consists of twelve pages, the first of which is numbered "2" by Reynolds. In other words, the first page of the revised version has not survived. The last two and a half pages of the revised version are given over to comments on Goldsmith's writing. There is little doubt that what Sir Joshua would have sent to the printer is the revised version in a somewhat more polished

[1] *See below*, p. 78.

form. There is no doubt at all that readers of the twentieth century would be the losers if this version were all that was printed, since many remarks which appear only in the earlier draft or in rough notes help to round out the picture. Accordingly the text here given is a composite, including, with trifling exceptions noted below, everything which Sir Joshua wrote on the subject. The structure of the sketch is that which is revealed in the revised version. Into this version have been woven the random notes and the sentences and paragraphs of the rough draft. The disadvantage of this method is that it necessarily results in a certain amount of repetition, but the repetition serves to emphasise what the author took most pains to write, and our interest in what Reynolds thought of Goldsmith makes any omission unthinkable. One anecdote, which could not be placed in the essay proper, has been included in this introduction. It is the story Reynolds had from Ridge concerning Goldsmith's improvidence. Otherwise the only omissions are a few phrases which are repeated verbatim elsewhere in the text and a few connectives which in the present arrangement would merely confuse the reader. Passages which Sir Joshua deleted have been restored to the text when they add information to the account.

REYNOLDS ON GOLDSMITH

THOSE only are the favourite characters of a biographer in which are united qualities which seem incompatible with each other, which appear impossible to exist together at the same time and in the same person. The writer reigns here and revels.[1] An opportunity is presented to him of displaying his sagacity and those nicer powers of discriminating between things which to an ordinary observer appear to have no marks of distinction, as well as of reconciling seeming contradictions. If anyone thinks that Dr. Goldsmith was a man not worth the investigation, we must refer him to the public advertisements, where he will find the booksellers have lived upon his reputation, as his friends have lived upon his character, ever since his death.

The literary world seemed to deplore his death more than could be expected, when it is considered how small a part of his works were wrote for fame; yet epigrams, epitaphs and monodies to his memory were without end. And what is still a greater proof of his popularity, the booksellers still continue to live upon his name, which they shamefully prostitute by prefixing it to works which he never saw, and which were probably written since his death.

Dr. Goldsmith's genius is universally acknowledged. All

[1] Writing to Burke in 1781 from Düsseldorf, Sir Joshua remarked: "Rubens reigns here and revels." The phrase is from *Paradise Lost*, IV, 765.

that we shall endeavour to do is to show what indeed is self-apparent, that such a genius could not be a fool or such a weak man as many people thought him.

Dr. Goldsmith was, in the truest as the most common sense of the word, a man of genius. But if we take the popular opinion of genius—that it is a gift, or supernatural power, entirely distinct from wisdom, knowledge, learning, and judgment, and that all these acquisitions contribute to destroy, rather than increase, the operations of genius—the Doctor must be acknowledged to have in this sense greater claim to the name of genius than any other man whatever, not excepting M. La Fontaine.[1] I do not mean that the Doctor entirely wanted all these qualities, but he appeared to want them in conversation.

Among those, therefore, who knew him but superficially, many suspected he was not the author of his own works, whilst others pronounced him an idiot inspired.[2] The

[1] "The curious personal character of La Fontaine, like that of some other men of letters, has been enshrined in a kind of legend by literary tradition. At an early age his absence of mind and indifference to business gave a subject to Tallemant des Réaux. His later contemporaries helped to swell the tale, and the eighteenth century finally accepted it, including the anecdotes of his meeting his son, being told who he was, and remarking, 'Ah, yes, I thought I had seen him somewhere'; of his insisting on fighting a duel with a supposed admirer of his wife and then imploring him to visit at his house just as before; of his going into company with his stocking wrong side out; with, for a contrast, those of his awkwardness and silence, if not positive rudeness, in company" (*Encyclopædia Britannica* under *La Fontaine*).

[2] Boswell in a note to the *Life of Johnson* writes: "Mr. Horace Walpole, who admired his writings, said he was 'an inspired idiot'." Tom Davies seems to have been the first to attribute the remark to Walpole, but not until 1781 in the third edition of his *Life of Garrick*. That Walpole made the remark cannot be proved, though similar expressions appear in his letters.

supposition that he did not write his own works had a great appearance of probability to those who knew him but superficially, but whoever knew him intimately and still continued of that opinion, it would reflect no great compliment to his sagacity. His more intimate acquaintances easily perceived his absurdities proceeded from other causes than from a feebleness of intellect, and that his follies were not those of a fool.

A great part of Dr. Goldsmith's folly and absurdity proceeded from principle, and partly from a want of early acquaintance with that life to which his reputation afterwards introduced him.

The author was intimately acquainted with Dr. Goldsmith. They unbosomed their minds freely to each other, not only in regard to the characters of their friends, but what contributed to make men's company desired or avoided. It was agreed that it was not superior parts, or wisdom, or knowledge that made men beloved—that men do not go into company with a desire of receiving instruction, but to be amused—that people naturally avoid that society where their minds are to be kept on the stretch.

He was of a sociable disposition. He had a very strong desire, which I believe nobody will think very peculiar or culpable, to be liked, to have his company sought after by his friends. To this end, for it was a system, he abandoned his respectable character as a writer or a man of observation to that of a character which nobody was afraid of being humiliated in his presence. This was his general principle, but at times, observing the attention paid to the conversation of others who

Goldsmith

Those only are the favorite Characters of
a Biographer in which are united qualities
which seem incompatable with each other
which appear impossible to exist together
at the same time or in the same person
the Writer reigns here & revels an
opportunity is presented to him of displaying his sagacity and those nicer
powers of discriminating between
things which to an ordinary observer
appear to have no marks of distinction
as well as of reconciling seeming contradictions

If any one thinks that Dr Goldsmith
of whom we are now about to speak
was a man not worth the investigation
we must referr him to the public advertisements not only of his real works
where the booksellers
have lived
upon his reputation as
his friends have lived upon his
character ever since his death

FIRST PAGE OF SIR JOSHUA'S CHARACTER SKETCH OF GOLDSMITH

"I am forced to write in a great hurry, and have little time for polishing my style."—REYNOLDS

spoke with more premeditation, and the neglect of himself though greedy and impatient to speak, he then resolved to be more formal and to carry his character about with him. But as he found he could not unite both, he naturally relaxed into his old manner, and which manner, it must be acknowledged, met with all success for the purposes he intended it.

The Doctor came late into the great world. He had lived a great part of his life with mean people. All his old habits were against him. It was too late to learn new ones, or at least for the new to sit easy on him. However, he set furiously about it. For one week he took one for a model and for another week [another].[1] This disadvantage, joined to an anxious desire and impatience to distinguish himself, brought him often into ridiculous situations. As he thought, and not without reason, that he had distinguished himself by his writings, he imagined therefore he ought at all times and in all places to be equally distinguished from the rest of the company, which, if neglected, he thought it incumbent on him to do that little service for himself. Without therefore waiting for a fit opportunity, he always took care to stand forward and draw the attention of the company upon himself. He talked without knowledge, not so much for the sake of shining[2] as [from] an impatience of neglect by being left out of the conversation.

[1] According to Boswell, "he had sagacity enough to cultivate assiduously the acquaintance of Johnson, and his faculties were gradually enlarged by the contemplation of such a model. To me and many others it appeared that he studiously copied the manner of Johnson, though, indeed, upon a smaller scale."

[2] "Goldsmith", said Johnson, "should not be for ever attempting to shine in conversation." "Goldsmith, as usual," wrote Boswell, "endeavoured, with too much eagerness, to *shine*."

He would therefore, to draw the attention of the company upon [himself], sing, stand upon his head, [or] dance about the room.[1]

His *Traveller* produced an eagerness unparalleled to see the author.[2] He was sought after with greediness. He knew much was expected from him. He had not that kind of prudence to take refuge in silence. He would speak on subjects [of] which he had not thought, and of which he was ignorant; he was impatient of being overlooked; he wished to be the principal figure in every group. Goldsmith having adopted this mode of conduct forgot that he must with the advantages accept of all the disadvantages that belonged to it. But he envied Johnson. It may easily be conceived what absurdity of conduct he must fall into in whom this restless desire predominates.

No man's company was ever more greedily sought after, for in his company the ignorant and illiterate were not only easy and free from any mortifying restraint, but even their vanity was gratified to find so admirable a writer so much upon a level, or inferior to themselves, in the arts of conversation.[3]

[1] " 'Sir, he is so much afraid of being unnoticed, that he often talks merely lest you should forget that he is in the company.' BOSWELL. 'Yes, he stands forward.' JOHNSON. 'True, Sir; but if a man is to stand forward, he should wish to do it not in an awkward posture, not in rage, not so as that he shall only be exposed to ridicule.' "

[2] "Goldsmith", said Johnson, "was a plant that flowered late." "Goldsmith being mentioned, Johnson observed that it was long before his merit came to be acknowledged. That he once complained to him, in ludicrous terms of distress, 'Whenever I write any thing, the public *make a point* to know nothing about it'; but that his *Traveller* brought him into high reputation."

[3] "When people," said Johnson, "find a man of the most distinguished abilities as a writer, their inferior while he is with them, it must be highly gratifying to them. What Goldsmith comically says of himself is very true—he always gets the better when he argues alone."

The ingenious and the learned, who wished to display their knowledge, were sure to find an opportunity of gratifying their desire by the triumph of refuting his paradoxes. And it must be acknowledged that he often fought like a tiger, and like the tiger he fought when turned on his back. He risked every opinion which that moment came into his head.

He was impatient when praises were bestowed on any person, however remote these might be from interfering with his own department. It was enough for him if they filled the mouths of men, to oppose their pretensions.

With this fighting, absurdity, and ridiculous kind of envy, he made always a sort of bustle, and wherever he was there was no yawning. The conversation never stagnated or languished. The same company [that], the moment he had turned his back, were in open cry on his absurdity and folly, were still desirous of meeting him again the next day.

He considered him as a friend indeed who would ask him to tell a story or sing a song, either of which requests he was always very ready to comply with, and very often without being asked, and without any preparation, to the great amazement of the company. His favourite songs were *Johnny Armstrong*, *Barbara Allen*, and *Death and the Lady*.[1] In singing the last he endeavoured to humour the dialogue by looking very fierce and speaking in a very rough voice for Death, which he

[1] In a letter to a kinsman written in 1757 Goldsmith says: "If I go to the opera where Signora Columba pours out all the mazes of melody, I sit and sigh for Lishoy fireside, and *Johnny Armstrong's Last Good Night* from Peggy Golden." Farmer Williams in *The Vicar* (chap. XVIII) could raise one's spirits by singing *Death and the Lady*.

suddenly changed when he came to the lady's part, putting on what he fancied to be a lady-like sweetness of countenance with a thin, shrill voice. His skill in singing those ballads was no ways superior to the professors of this art which are heard every day in the streets, but whilst he was thus employed he was a conspicuous figure at least and was relieved from that horror which he entertained of being overlooked by the company.

It must be confessed that whoever excelled in any art or science, however different from his own, was sure to be considered by him as a rival. It was sufficient that he was an object of praise, as if he thought that the world had but a certain quantity of that commodity to give away, and what was bestowed upon others made less come to his share.[1] This odious quality, however, was not so disagreeable in him as it generally is in other people. It was so far from being of that black malignant kind which excites hatred and disgust, that it was, from its being so artless and obvious, only ridiculous.

The following happened once in a large company, which may serve as an instance to characterise the Doctor's manner. Somebody said that one of Mr. Garrick's excellencies, amongst many others, was his powers in telling of a story. This being universally agreed to, excited the Doctor's envy.

[1] "Sir Joshua used to say," wrote Northcote, "that Goldsmith looked at, or considered, public notoriety, or fame, as one great parcel, to the whole of which he laid claim, and whoever partook of any part of it, whether dancer, singer, sleight of hand man, or tumbler, deprived him of his right, and drew off the attention of the world from himself, and which he was striving to gain."

"I do not see what difficulty there can be in telling a story well. I would undertake to tell a story as well as Mr. Garrick, and I will tell you one now, and I will do my best.[1] There lived a cobbler—some people do laugh at this story and some do not; however, the story is this—there lived a cobbler in a stall. This stall was opposite our house, so I knew him very well. This cobbler a bailie came after, for I must tell you he was a very low fellow."

("But you was acquainted with him, you say. He used to be often at your house.")

"Ay, he used to come over to fetch our shoes when they wanted mending, but not as an acquaintance. I always kept the best company."

("Go on with your story, Doctor.")

"This cobbler was afraid of being arrested.——Why, the very best company used to come in our house. Squire Thomson used to dine with us, who was one of the first men in the country. I remember his coach and six, which we used to see come galloping down the hill, and then my mother, who was a little woman, was quite hid at the head of the table behind a great sirloin of beef. You could but just see the top of her head."

("Well, but go on, Doctor Goldsmith, with your story.")

"When the bailie came to, and knocked at, the door of the cobbler's stall in order to have it opened, the cobbler,

[1] Once when Johnson was in his friend Hoole's coach and the coachman had been ordered to drive as rapidly as possible, Johnson "put his head out of one of the windows to see they were going right, and rubbing his hands with an air of satisfaction exclaimed—'This man drives fast and well; were Goldsmith here now he would tell us he could do better.' "

being aware, answered in the voice of a child (here the Doctor changes his voice), 'Put in your finger into the hole and lift up the latch,' which as soon as he had done, the cobbler with his knife cut the finger off, and still speaking in the child's voice, 'Put in the other finger, Sir, if you please.' "

The Doctor's folly, freaks, and nonsense, though there was seldom anything in it which marked it to be the nonsense of a man of genius, yet neither had it any of those marks of feebleness by which weakness and ignorance is immediately discovered. If he was sometimes foolish out of season, he never was what is worse, wise out of season. For instance, Dr. Goldsmith never made common observations with the air and as if he had spoke oracles, or ever acquiesced in what others advanced, in order to conceal his own ignorance. On the contrary, he delighted in advancing paradoxes,[1] and opposed others with false authorities, by which he often indeed discovered his ignorance, but not weakness. (The sterlings.)[2]

Goldsmith had no wit in conversation, but to do him justice, he did not much attempt it. When in company with ladies he was always endeavouring after humour, and as continually failed; but his ill success was equally diverting to the company

[1] "Goldsmith", wrote Boswell, "attempted this evening to maintain, I suppose from an affectation of paradox, 'that knowledge was not desirable on its own account, for it often was a source of unhappiness.' "

[2] The words in round brackets are apparently Sir Joshua's note to himself to include at this point an example of what he has just said. My guess is that Reynolds had in mind the following passage in the *History of the Earth and Animated Nature*: "The under jaw in man possesses a great variety of motions; while the upper has been thought, by many, to be quite immovable. However, that it moves in man a very easy experiment will suffice to convince us. If we keep the head fixed, with any thing between our teeth—the edge of a table, for

as if he had succeeded. If they laughed, he was happy and did not seem to care whether it was with him or at him.[1] But when he was in company with the philosophers, he was grave, wise, and very inclinable to dispute established opinions. This immediately produced a general cry. Every man had arguments of confutation ready, and he himself was at once placed in the situation he so much loved, of being the object of attention of the whole company. However this disposition to paradoxes might be sometimes troublesome, it often called out the rest of the company into conversation, and as has been often observed, wherever the Doctor was, the conversation was never known to languish.

What Goldsmith intended for humour was purposely repeated as serious. (Malagrida.)[2] However, to do justice to

---

instance—and then open our mouths, we shall find that both jaws recede from it at the same time; the upper jaw rises and the lower falls, and the table remains untouched between them. The upper jaw, therefore, has motion as well as the under." This was one of the most talked-of blunders in the book, even before it had been published. Goldsmith's note on the first sentence quoted above reads: "Mr. Buffon is of this opinion. He says that the upper jaw is immovable in all animals whatsoever. However, the parrot is an obvious exception; and so is man himself, as shown above." The same statement appears later in the chapter on parrots. I suggest that Sir Joshua, thinking of talking birds, wrote *sterlings* [i.e., starlings] rather than parrots.

[1] Compare Boswell's lines on himself:

> So not a bent sixpence cares he
> Whether with him or at him you laugh.

[2] Here Reynolds planned to introduce the most famous of Goldsmith's alleged blunders. Lord Shelburne had acquired the nickname of Malagrida after a Jesuit of that name who had been executed on a charge of heresy. Shelburne's duplicity in politics had led the King to call him the "Jesuit of Berkeley Square". Seated next to him at the theatre, Goldsmith said to him, "Do you know that I never could conceive the reason why they call you Malagrida, for Malagrida was a very good sort of man."

the world, a man seldom acquires the character of absurd without deserving it. As the *bons mots* of other wits are handed about the town, the Doctor's blunders and absurdities, circulated with equal success, helped to increase his fame and give everybody a desire of seeing the man, and this perhaps not without some mixture of self-congratulation to find a person whom they were obliged to look up to for superior talent sink below their own level when in conversation.

Goldsmith's mind was entirely unfurnished. When he was engaged in a work, he had all his knowledge to find, which when he found, he knew how to use, but forgot it immediately after he had used it.

He was so far from exciting envy in others by any exhibition of his own superior powers in extempore thinking that he would in a shorter time write the poem in his closet than give a satisfactory account in company of the plan or conduct of the work, or give any satisfactory explanation of a passage.[1] This reminds me of a story of two sculptors who were rival candidates for a great work which was to be given to the most able artist. They were desired, by those who were appointed to be the judges of their respective merit, to speak upon their art with regard to their intention. After one of them had finished his

[1] "Chamier once asked him," said Johnson, "what he meant by *slow*, the last word in the first line of *The Traveller*:

'Remote, unfriended, melancholy, slow.'

Did he mean tardiness of locomotion? Goldsmith, who would say something without consideration, answered 'Yes'. I was sitting by, and said, 'No, Sir; you do not mean tardiness of locomotion; you mean that sluggishness of mind which comes upon a man in solitude.' Chamier believed then that I had written the line as much as if he had seen me write it."

speech with all the ostentation of eloquence, when it came to his rival's turn to speak, who had not the same gift of elocution, though a better sculptor, he only said, "What this man *says* I can *do*."

Perhaps one of the reasons why the Doctor was so very inexpert in explaining even the principles of his own art was his ignorance of the scholastic or technical terms by which similar things are distinguished. He professed himself an enemy to all those investigations which he said did not at all increase the powers of doing, but only enabled a person to talk about it, of those researches of which you receive the full result and advantage without study or attention equal to those who had spent their life in the pursuit. He considered this as superfluous and needless a science as that which was taught the *bourgeois gentilhomme*, who was persuaded he had made a great proficiency in rhetoric when he knew the operation of the organs of speech, or, as he himself says, what he did when he said *u*.[1]

No man ever wrote so much from his feelings as Dr. Goldsmith. I do not mean here the vulgar opinion of being

[1] The passage in Molière's play to which Reynolds refers was thus translated by Ravenscroft:

"JORDEN. Do you know what it is you do when you say *U*?

LUCIA. I say *U*.

JOR. Pish—but what do you do then? Come, say *U*.

LUC. Well, Sir, *U*.

JOR. Well, what did you do then?

LUC. I did as you bid me.

JOR. Invincible stupidity, you opened your mouth, thrust your lips out at length forward, let your under jaw fall almost to meet the upper, and strongly sent out your breath—*U*—see there—*U*—as it were, make a mouth at one—*U*——"

possessed himself with the passion which he wished to excite. I mean only that he governed himself by an internal feeling of the right rather than by any written rules of art. He judged, for instance, by his ear, whether the verse was musical, without caring or perhaps knowing whether it would bear examination by the rules of the *prosodia*.

He felt with great exactness, far above what words can teach, the propriety in composition, how one sentiment breeds another in the mind, preferring this as naturally to grow out of the preceding and rejecting another, though more brilliant, as breaking the chain of ideas. In short, he felt by a kind of instinct or intuition all those nice discriminations which to grosser minds appear to have no difference. This instinct is real genius if anything can be so called. But little of this judgment, as was before observed, appeared in conversation. It came when he took up the pen and quitted him when he laid it down.[1] Even his friends did not think him capable of marking with so much sagacity and precision the predominant and striking features of their characters as he did in the epitaphs.

These were the excellencies and the defects of the author of *The Traveller* and *The Deserted Village*, two of the most excellent works in the English language.

His name as a poet must depend upon the quality, not the quantity, of his works. *The Traveller*, *The Deserted Village*, the

[1] "No man," remarked Johnson, "was more foolish when he had not a pen in his hand, or more wise when he had."

ballad in the *Vicar of Wakefield*, his two comedies (*The Good-Natured Man* and *She Stoops to Conquer*), and if to these we add his epitaphs on his friends, they make all his works in poetry which he owned.

His *Traveller* alone would have entitled him to a place in the Poets' Corner.[1] It is a small, well-polished gem, the work of many years. It was begun when he was abroad and retouched at different periods since, and is more completely finished than any of his other works. There is a general commanding air of grandeur that pervades the whole, that never sinks into languor. The general and popular character of each nation is strongly marked.

He is very sparing of epithets, which though they give a richness destroy simplicity, which I think is the peculiar characteristic of his poetry.[2]

His works in prose were *The History of England in Letters from a Father to his Son*, which the booksellers endeavour to pass upon the world as the work of the late Lord Lyttelton,

[1] Sir Joshua annotates this: "A monument for Dr. Goldsmith is now making by Mr. Nollekens, the expense of which will be defrayed by a subscription among his friends." Northcote reports that Sir Joshua "went himself to Westminster Abbey, and fixed upon the place where Goldsmith's monument now stands, over a door in the Poets' Corner. He thought himself lucky in being able to find so conspicuous a situation for it, as there scarcely remained another so good".

[2] "It is remarkable," cried Mr. Burchell, "that both the poets you mention [Gay and Ovid] have equally contributed to introduce a false taste into their respective countries, by loading all their lines with epithet. Men of little genius found them most easily imitated in their defects, and English poetry, like that in the latter empire of Rome, is nothing at present but a combination of luxuriant images, without plot or connection; a string of epithets that improve the sound without carrying on the sense" (*The Vicar*, chap. VIII).

The State of Polite Literature in Europe, *Chinese Tales*, a periodical paper called *The Bee*, *The Life of Mr. Beau Nash of Bath*, *The Life of Dr. Parnell*, the *Vicar of Wakefield*, a novel, *The Roman History* in [two] volumes, *The English History* in [four] volumes, and *The History of Animated Nature* in [eight] volumes.

Of his style in prose we may venture to say he was never languid, tedious, or insipid. It is always sprightly and animated. He very well knew the art of captivating the attention of the reader, both by his choice of matter and the lively narration with which it is accompanied.

IV

JOHNSON AND REYNOLDS

§ 1

By common consent in his own day Sir Joshua was regarded as the supreme authority on matters Johnsonian. Even Boswell called him "master of the subject", and in the dedication of the *Life* addressed him as "the intimate and beloved friend of that great man; the friend whom he declared to be 'the most invulnerable man he knew; whom, if he should quarrel with him, he should find the most difficulty how to abuse'. You, my dear Sir, studied him and knew him well, you venerated and admired him. Yet, luminous as he was upon the whole, you perceived all the shades which mingled in the grand composition, all the little peculiarities and slight blemishes which marked the literary Colossus".

The story of their first meeting is well known, but like many well-known stories the facts in the case are suspect. Under the date 1752 Boswell writes: "When Johnson lived in Castle Street, Cavendish Square, he used frequently to visit two ladies who lived opposite to him, Miss Cotterells, daughters of Admiral Cotterell. Reynolds used also to visit there, and thus they met. Mr. Reynolds . . . had, from the first reading of his *Life of Savage*, conceived a very high admiration of Johnson's powers of writing. His conversation no less delighted him, and he cultivated his acquaintance with the laudable zeal of one who was ambitious of general improvement. Sir Joshua, indeed, was lucky enough at their very first meeting to make a remark which was so much above the commonplace style of conversation, that Johnson at once perceived that Reynolds had the habit of thinking for himself. The ladies were regretting the death of a friend to whom they owed great obligations; upon which Reynolds observed, 'You have, however, the comfort of being relieved from a burden of gratitude.' They were shocked a little at this alleviating suggestion, as too selfish; but Johnson defended it in his clear and forcible manner and was much pleased with the *mind*, the fair view of human nature, which it exhibited, like some of the reflections of Rochefoucauld. The consequence was that he went home with Reynolds and supped with him."

Soon after the *Life* was published, Mrs. Lewis, one of the two Cotterell sisters, criticised this story because of "the many mistakes both as to time and circumstance". If we may trust her account, the Cotterells did not meet Johnson until, at the earliest, 1754—sixteen years after he had left Castle Street. It was, she says, above a year after that when Reynolds was introduced to her sister. Of course Mrs. Lewis's memory after thirty-five years may have deceived her, but I am inclined to accept her version, which fits in with the hypothesis that the two men first met in 1756. It should be added, in justice to Boswell, that he dated the meeting on the authority of Francis Barber and described what happened at the meeting as Sir Joshua remembered it. On 14 June 1786, Boswell had called on Mrs. Lewis and questioned her, but was unable to get any information from her. In the light of this, her criticism of Boswell's inaccuracies would seem to be ungenerous.

In 1755 Johnson had published his *Dictionary*, and as author of *The Vanity of Human Wishes* and of *The Rambler* was already regarded as the dominant writer of the day. It would be natural to assume, therefore, that young Reynolds was flattered at attracting his attention and must have done what he could to cement a friendship with him. On the contrary, if Northcote is correct, Reynolds was at first annoyed by Johnson's visits. "He frequently called in the evening and remained to a late hour, when Mr. Reynolds was desirous of going into new company, after having been harassed by his professional occupations the whole day. This sometimes overcame his patience to such a degree, that, one evening in particular, on entering the room where Johnson was waiting to see him, he immediately took up his hat and went out of the house. Reynolds

SAMUEL JOHNSON, BY REYNOLDS

"I found that I had a very perfect idea of Johnson's figure from the portrait of him painted by Sir Joshua Reynolds soon after he had published his *Dictionary*, in the attitude of sitting in his easy chair in deep meditation."—BOSWELL

hoped by this means he would have been effectually cured; but Johnson still persisted and at last gained his friendship."

They had not known each other long before Johnson was sitting for the first of at least five portraits. It was completed early in 1757 and remained in the painter's house until, many years later, it was given to Boswell, who caused it to be engraved as the frontispiece to the *Life*.

There is no need here to describe in detail the friendship of Johnson and Reynolds. Suffice it to say that it was based on mutual love and respect. What Johnson wrote, Reynolds read with something like awe (*Rasselas* was "writ by an angel"). What Johnson said in conversation, Reynolds listened to as to an oracle ("he qualified my mind to think justly"). Johnson for his part admired Sir Joshua's mental powers ("when Reynolds tells me something, I consider myself as possessed of an idea the more") and his good judgment ("I am always proud of your approbation"). While visiting in the country in the summer of 1764, Johnson heard that Reynolds had been ill and wrote to him a letter which is now in the Hyde Collection. In it he says: "If the amusement of my company can exhilarate the languor of a slow recovery, I will not delay a day to come to you; for I know not how I can so effectually promote my own pleasure as by pleasing you, or my own interest as by preserving you, in whom, if I should lose you, I should lose almost the only man whom I call a friend."

Of the many notes which Sir Joshua must have written to Johnson only two have hitherto been known to survive, one asking Johnson to look over what Reynolds had been writing, the other referring to an invitation from Miss Monckton. A third note has turned up in the Boswell Papers, and this too concerns an engagement with Miss Monckton. Mary Monckton, later Countess of Cork and Orrery, was one of the outstanding bluestockings of the day. In 1782 she was, wrote Fanny Burney, "between thirty and forty, very short, very fat, but handsome; splendidly and fantastically dressed, rouged not unbecomingly, yet evidently and palpably desirous of gaining notice and admiration." She was one of Johnson's favourites. According to Boswell, her "vivacity enchanted the Sage, and they used to talk together with all imaginable ease. A singular instance happened one evening, when she insisted that some of Sterne's writings were very pathetic. Johnson bluntly denied it. 'I am sure (said she) they have affected *me.*' 'Why (said Johnson, smiling and rolling himself about), that is, because, dearest, you're a dunce.' When she some time afterwards mentioned this to him, he said with equal truth and politeness, 'Madam, if I had thought so, I certainly should not have said it.' "

Sir Joshua was a regular attendant at her brilliant parties. Her name frequently appears in his engagement-books, often coupled with Johnson's. "Miss Monckton, 8, and to speak to Dr. Johnson." The note which follows was probably written in 1782.

> Sir Joshua Reynolds's compliments to Dr. Johnson. He has sent word that he will wait on Miss Monckton on Saturday. Sir Joshua will send his coach or call himself on Dr. Johnson a little before eight.
>
> Leicester Fields, May 3rd.

I do not know whether it has been pointed out that Johnson refrained from abbreviating Sir Joshua's name when speaking of him. Boswell tells us that "Johnson had a way of contracting the names of his friends; as, Beauclerk, Beau; Boswell, Bozzy; Langton, Lanky; Murphy, Mur; Sheridan, Sherry. I remember one day, when Tom Davies was telling that Dr. Johnson said, 'We are all in labour for a name to *Goldy's* play,' Goldsmith seemed displeased that such a liberty should be taken with his name, and said, 'I have often desired him not to call me *Goldy*.' " *Renny* was the name he reserved for Sir Joshua's sister Frances. To the best of my knowledge Reynolds was "Mr. Reynolds" to him until knighted, "Sir Joshua" thereafter. Since we know that the two were intimate, it looks as if he did this to show respect for his friend.

Sir Joshua returned the compliment, if compliment it was. Northcote told Hazlitt that Reynolds was somewhat like a Quaker in that he never flattered the Great, "never even gave them their proper titles. I never heard the words *your lordship* or *your ladyship* come from his mouth; nor did he ever say *Sir* in speaking to any one but Dr. Johnson; and when he did not hear distinctly what the latter said (which often happened) he would then say 'Sir?' that he might repeat it."

The instances which reflect anything like friction between the two are hard to find. Johnson told Thrale in 1775 that Reynolds had not read *Taxation no Tyranny*. "I never look at his pictures, so he won't read my writings." At the same period he wrote to Boswell: "Reynolds has taken too much to strong liquor, and seems to delight in his new character." Once, we know, there was a momentary clash, when Johnson, at the time a water-drinker, tried to end an argument by accusing Reynolds of being drunk. The version recorded in Boswell's journal differs slightly from that in the *Life*. Johnson "said to Sir Joshua, 'I won't argue any more with you. You're too far gone' (insinuating that he had drank too much). Sir Josh. very properly took fire a little and said, 'That, Sir, is a speech fitter for me, supposing me to be in the situation which you seem to allege.' 'Nay,' said Johnson. 'Don't be angry,' and calmed to courteousness." Against such mild criticisms one could place numerous compliments which have on them the stamp of sincerity. Here is a typical example. Boswell and Johnson are in a coach. "As we passed through Leicester Square I pointed to Sir Joshua Reynolds's house and said, 'There lives our friend.' 'Ay, Sir,' said the Doctor, 'there lives a very great man.' " And what Johnson gave to Reynolds, Reynolds returned with interest. In his letters and in his conversations he reveals his affection and admiration, but his fullest and most thoughtful commentary is to be found in the memoir here printed.

§ 2

There can be little doubt that Sir Joshua was writing this for Boswell and at Boswell's request. Nor is it difficult to establish rough dates for the time when Sir Joshua was putting his thoughts on paper.

In the summer of 1785 Boswell was in London preparing his

Hebridean journal for publication, and incidentally sitting to Reynolds for his portrait. The *Tour to the Hebrides* was not published until the first of October, but Reynolds was one of a few who received an advance copy on 21 September and who dined the next day with the author at Malone's, where the book was much applauded. Two days later Boswell departed for Scotland, leaving Malone in charge of preparing the second edition, which appeared shortly before Christmas.

On 26 September Sir Joshua wrote to the Duke of Rutland: "Mr. Boswell has just sent me his *Johnsoniana*, which is one of the most entertaining books I ever read." This sentiment is echoed in a letter which Malone wrote to Boswell on 5 October: "Sir J. R. has read the *Tour twice* over, and is very lavish in its praise." Later in the same letter he tells Boswell not to "forget Sir Joshua R's observation about Johnson's extraordinary motions not being *involuntary*, and therefore not exactly described". The reference is to a passage early in the *Tour* in which Boswell, when describing Johnson, had written: "He was frequently disturbed by cramps, or convulsive contractions, of the nature of that distemper called St. Vitus's dance." At this point in the second edition the following footnote was added: "Such they appeared to me; but since the former edition, Sir Joshua Reynolds has observed to me, 'that Dr. Johnson's extraordinary gestures were only habits, in which he indulged himself at certain times. When in company where he was not free, or when engaged earnestly in conversation, he never gave way to such habits, which proves that they were not involuntary.' I still however think, that these gestures were involuntary; for surely had not that been the case, he would have restrained them in the public streets." What lies behind this note and elucidates the memoir is revealed in the Boswell Papers.

When the book was being discussed at Malone's on 22 September, Reynolds must have singled out this passage, disagreed with it, and expressed his own theory. Malone, planning the second edition, reminded Boswell of the fact and suggested that the passage be rewritten. Boswell replied on 13 October that he was pleased with Sir Joshua's approbation, but refused to accept the alternate theory.

Meanwhile Malone wrote a note (probably the one printed above), embodying Sir Joshua's idea, and sent it to Reynolds for approval. On 19 October Malone reported to Boswell: "He approved, but sent me a much longer and very valuable discussion of the subject, which I shall enclose with this letter. It would not have been got in without a good deal of trouble; besides I thought it too valuable to be thrown away and better to be reserved for the *Life*. His solution of the starting and gestures being connected with ideas from which he shrunk, is surely very ingenious."

What Malone enclosed is the following note, written in Sir Joshua's hand, but written as though by Boswell. The words in italics are deleted in the manuscript.

> *Such they appeared to me, but since the former edition Sir Joshua Reynolds has observed to me that* those motions or tricks of Dr. Johnson are improperly called convulsions. He could sit motionless, when he was told so to do, as well as any other man. His opinion is that it proceeded from a habit he had indulged himself in of accompanying his thoughts with certain untoward actions, and that those actions always appeared to him as if they were meant to reprobate some part of his past conduct. Whenever he was not engaged in conversation, such thoughts were sure to rush into his mind; and for this reason any company, any employment whatever, he preferred to being alone. The great business of his life, he said, was to escape from himself. This disposition he considered as the disease of his mind, which nothing cured but company.
>
> One instance of his absence and particularity, as it is characteristic of the man, may be worth relating. When he and the Doctor took a journey together into the West, they visited the late Mr. Bankes of Dorsetshire. The conversation

> turning upon pictures, which Johnson could not well see, he retired to a corner of the room, stretching out his right leg as far as he could reach before him, then bringing up his left leg and stretching his right still further on. The old gentleman observing him, went up to him, and in a very courteous manner assured him that though it was not a new house, the flooring was perfectly safe. The Doctor started from his reverie, like a person waked out of his sleep, but spoke not a word.

Boswell liked the note and agreed with Malone that it should not be buried as a footnote to a revised edition of the *Tour*. "The *contractions*," he replies on 27 October, "are well stated for the present. Sir Joshua's note at *large* will be admirable in the *Life*." As an afterthought he adds: "But it must be in Sir Joshua's own name." Accordingly in the *Life* the account reads in the first person, *his* becomes *my*, *him* becomes *me*, &c. Malone's decision resulted in acquiring good "copy" for the *Life* and at the same time enriching the new edition of the *Tour* by a paraphrase. Thus Boswell ate his cake and had it too.

At the end of the *Tour* the *Life* is advertised as "Preparing for the Press". Reynolds is one of those there named as having contributed materials for it. These materials cannot now be identified. One contribution which may have already been made concerns the note that Pope wrote after Johnson had published his *London*. Other contributions, Johnson's letters and certain anecdotes, were acquired by Boswell at later dates. On 20 February 1786, for example, Boswell "wrote some anecdotes of Dr. Johnson dictated by Sir Joshua". Nowhere is there any mention of Sir Joshua's memoir, nor is it likely that Boswell ever saw what has survived. Otherwise we should have expected it to have become a part of Boswell's archives. As I have pointed out elsewhere, some of the phrases and some of the anecdotes which are found in the memoir also appear in the *Life*. Conceivably Sir Joshua turned over to Boswell a fair copy which has not survived. Possibly in his memoir he merely recorded what he had already dictated to Boswell. All that can be said with assurance is that Sir Joshua would not have been writing the memoir for anyone but Boswell, that it was probably written in 1786 or 1787, and that some of the materials in it were incorporated in the *Life*. The manuscript in its incomplete form remained in Sir Joshua's home until his death and in the possession of his family for another two generations.

§ 3

The key to an understanding of Dr. Johnson, according to Reynolds, was his fear of being alone. His "vile melancholy" imperilled his sanity. Sir Joshua refers specifically to the first three paragraphs of Chapter XLIV of *Rasselas*, in which Imlac discourses on "the dangerous prevalence of imagination".

" 'Disorders of intellect,' answered Imlac, 'happen much more often than superficial observers will easily believe. Perhaps if we speak with rigorous exactness, no human mind is in its right state. There is no man whose imagination does not sometimes predominate over his reason, who can regulate his attention wholly by his will, and whose ideas will come and go at his command. No man will be found in whose mind airy notions do not sometimes tyrannise and force him to hope or fear beyond the limits of sober probability. All power of fancy over reason is a degree of insanity; but while this power is such as we can control and repress, it is not visible to others nor considered as any depravation of the mental faculties. It is not pronounced madness but when it becomes ungovernable and apparently influences speech or action.

" 'To indulge the power of fiction and send imagination out upon the wing, is often the sport of those who delight too much in silent speculation. When we are alone we are not always busy; the labour of excogitation is too violent to last long; the ardour of inquiry will sometimes give way to idleness or satiety. He who has nothing external that can divert him, must find pleasure in his own thoughts, and must conceive himself what he is not: for who is pleased with what he is? He then expatiates in boundless futurity, and culls from all imaginable conditions that which for the present moment he should most desire, amuses his desires with impossible enjoyments, and confers upon his pride unattainable dominion. The mind dances from scene to scene, unites all pleasures in all combinations, and riots in delights which nature and fortune, with all their bounty, cannot bestow.

" 'In time some particular train of ideas fixes the attention; all other intellectual gratifications are rejected; the mind in weariness or leisure recurs constantly to the favourite conception, and feasts on the luscious falsehood whenever she is offended with the bitterness of truth. By degrees the reign of fancy is confirmed; she grows first imperious and in time despotic. Then fictions begin to operate as realities, false opinions fasten upon the mind, and life passes in dreams of rapture or of anguish.

" 'This, Sir, is one of the dangers of solitude. . . .' "

Sir Joshua's memoir is not a rambling series of anecdotes, held together merely because everything pertains to Johnson. It is a word-portrait, and the passage just quoted points up the unity of that portrait. Because he feared solitude Johnson was always in company. Because he was always in company he became an experienced conversationalist. In a sense the conversation was the man, and Sir Joshua paints the portrait by defining and describing his friend's conversational abilities.

Boswell once praised Johnson for his skill in drawing characters. "He is undoubtedly admirable in this," replied Reynolds, "but in order to mark the characters which he draws, he overcharges them and gives people more than they really have, whether of good or bad." The character of Johnson which Reynolds draws is not overcharged. It is a controlled piece of writing, a patently honest attempt to portray his friend as he saw him. It is in writing of this sort, rather than in the formal discourses which he published, that we can see the author as others have described him. With modesty and fair-mindedness he penetrates to the essential Johnson. In so doing he reveals not only Johnson but himself.

§ 4

As has been said earlier, the manuscript of this memoir was in the possession of Sir Joshua's collateral descendants as late as a hundred years ago. At that time it was seen and copied by Charles Robert Leslie, who included it in his biography of Reynolds. Leslie's version was reprinted and fully annotated by G. B. Hill in the second volume of his *Johnsonian Miscellanies* and has thus for over a half-century been readily available to interested readers. If Leslie's version had been reasonably complete and reasonably accurate there would be no need to attempt an improvement on Hill's well-annotated edition. But the facts are otherwise.

The manuscript, which is in my possession, consists of fourteen leaves, 12 × 7¾ inches in size. Some of these contain random notes concerning the subject. The rest are given over to a rough draft and a revision of that draft. The memoir was never completed. Leslie arranged the pages so as to give a more or less continuous narrative, but must have spent little time studying the manuscript. Certainly he does not present the material in the order indicated by Sir Joshua. Furthermore he was at times unable to decipher the handwriting and omitted a number of significant passages. When he writes: "I have transcribed the paper exactly, except in the matter of punctuation and in the introduction, now and then, of a word between brackets to complete the sense," he is, to put it bluntly, not telling the truth. How far his transcription departs from the original I have shown elsewhere.

The text here presented is a reading text, designed to supplant the one which Leslie has given. The method is that followed in preparing the text of the Goldsmith memoir. The only omissions are a few phrases or sentences which merely repeat what Reynolds wrote in another part of the memcir. Where he has provided alternate readings I have selected the one which I consider the more effective.

REYNOLDS ON JOHNSON

From thirty years' intimacy with Dr. Johnson I certainly have had the means, if I had equally the ability, of giving you a true and perfect idea of the character and peculiarities of this extraordinary man. The habits of my profession unluckily extend to the consideration of so much only of character as lies on the surface, as is expressed in the lineaments of the countenance. An attempt to go deeper and investigate the peculiar colouring of his mind, as distinguished from all other minds, nothing but your earnest desire can excuse the presumption even of attempting. Such as it is, you may make what use of it you please.

We are both of Dr. Johnson's school. For my own part I acknowledge the highest obligations to him. He may be said to have formed my mind and to have brushed off from it a deal of rubbish. Those very people whom he has taught to think rightly will occasionally criticise the opinions of their master when he nods, but we should always recollect that it is he himself who taught us and enabled us to do it.

Of his learning as grammarian his *English Dictionary* testifies. His skill in biography and criticism is shown in his *Lives of the English Poets*. His penetration and skill in developing the source of the passions, the human mind, is discovered in his moral essays. Of these acquisitions, superior as he was to all his contemporaries, I shall say nothing, but leave to others to give him that praise which he justly deserves. It is for higher qualities that he has acquired the esteem and respect of all men who respect piety and virtue.

I shall remark such qualities only as his works alone cannot convey, and among those the most distinguished was his possessing a mind which was, as I may say, always ready for use. Most general subjects had undoubtedly been already discussed in the course of a studious thinking life. In this respect few men ever came better prepared into whatever company chance might throw him, and the love which he had to society gave him a facility in the practice of applying his knowledge to the matter in hand which I believe was never exceeded by any man. It has been frequently observed that he was a singular instance of a man who had so much distinguished himself by his writings that his conversation not only supported his character as an author, which is very rarely seen, but what is still rarer, in the opinion of many was superior. Those who have lived with the wits of the age know how rarely this happens.

I have had the habit of thinking that this quality, as well as others of the same kind, are possessed in consequence of accidental circumstances attending his life.

What Dr. Johnson said a few days before his death of his disposition to insanity was no new discovery to those who were intimate with him. The character of Imlac in *Rasselas*, when the means of preventing madness is discussed, I always considered as a comment on his own conduct which he himself practised—and, as it now appears, very successfully, since we know he continued to possess his understanding in its full vigour to the last. In one of those extempore prayers which he frequently, a few days before his death,[1] poured out with great fervency, he thanked God for preserving his understanding unimpaired to the last, more especially as he always had through life a great disposition to insanity. This his friends must have remarked, and imputed to it the horror he had of being alone, and he never was if he could avoid it.

Solitude to him was horror; nor would he ever trust himself alone unemployed in writing or reading. He has often begged me to accompany him home with him to prevent his being alone in the coach. Any company to him was better than none; by which he connected himself with many mean persons whose presence he could command. And for this purpose he established a club at a little ale-house in Essex Street, composed of a strange mixture of very learned, very ingenious, and very odd people. Of the former was Dr. Heberden, Mr. Windham, Mr. Boswell, Mr. Steevens, Mr. Paradise; those of the latter sort I do not think proper to enumerate.[2] By thus living, by

[1] On the fifth of December, eight days before Johnson died, Reynolds was alone with him. This was perhaps the visit mentioned in a letter of Hannah More's: "He sent the other day for Sir Joshua; and after much serious conversation told him he had three favours to beg of him, and he hoped he would not refuse a dying friend, be they what they would. Sir Joshua promised. The first was that he would never paint on a Sunday; the second that he would forgive him thirty pounds that he had lent him, as he wanted to leave them to a distressed family; the third was that he would read the Bible whenever he had an opportunity, and that he would never omit it on a Sunday. There was no difficulty but upon the *first* point; but at length Sir Joshua promised to gratify him in all."

[2] Sir Joshua was asked to join this club, but refused, probably because of his dislike for James Barry, the artist. The mention of Barry in Johnson's letter to Sir Joshua (4 December 1783) shows that he expected trouble. "It is inconvenient to me to come out; I should else have waited on you with an account of a

SAMUEL JOHNSON

"The picture of him by Sir Joshua Reynolds, which was . . . scraped in mezzotint by Doughty, is extremely like him; there is in it that appearance of a labouring working mind, of an indolent reposing body, which he had to a very great degree."—HAWKINS

necessity, so much in company, more perhaps than any other studious man whatever, he had acquired by habit, and which habit alone can give, that facility, and we may add docility of mind, by which he was so much distinguished.

Another circumstance likewise contributed not a little to the powers which he had of expressing himself, which was a rule, which he said he always practised, of always on every occasion speaking his best, whether the person to whom he addressed himself was or was not capable of comprehending him.[1] "If," says he, "I am understood, my labour is not lost. If it is above their comprehension, there is some gratification, though it was the admiration of ignorance"; and those, he said, were the most sincere admirers; and quoted Baxter, who made a rule never to finish a sermon without saying something which

---

little evening club which we are establishing in Essex Street in the Strand, and of which you are desired to be one. It will be held at the Essex Head, now kept by an old servant of Thrale's. The company is numerous, and, as you will see by the list, miscellaneous. The terms are lax, and the expenses light. Mr. Barry was adopted by Dr. Brocklesby, who joined with me in forming the plan. We meet thrice a week, and he who misses forfeits twopence. If you are willing to become a member, draw a line under your name. Return the list. We meet for the first time on Monday at eight."

[1] "Dr. Johnson," wrote Malone, "is as correct and elegant in his common conversation as in his writings. He never seems to study either for thoughts or words; and is on all occasions so fluent, so well-informed, so accurate, and even eloquent, that I never left his company without regret. Sir Josh. Reynolds told me that from his first outset in life he had always had this character; and by what means he had attained it. He told him he had early laid it down, as a fixed rule, always to do his best, on *every occasion* and in *every company*, to impart whatever he knew in the best language he could put it in; and that by constant practice and never suffering any careless expression to escape him, or attempting to deliver his thoughts without arranging them in the clearest manner he could, it was now become habitual to him."

he knew was beyond the comprehension of his audience in order to insure their admiration.[1]

Dr. Johnson, by this continual practice, made that a habit which was at first an exertion; for every person who knew him must have observed that the moment he was left out of the conversation, either from his deafness or from whatever cause, he remained but a few minutes without speaking or listening. His mind appeared to be preying on itself; he fell into a reverie accompanied with strange antic gesticulations. But this was when his mind was absent; he never did when his mind was engaged by the conversation. It was therefore improperly called by Pope, as well as by others, convulsions, which imply involuntary contortions;[2] whereas, a word addressed to him,

[1] Boswell asked him what works of Richard Baxter's he should read. "He said, 'Read any of them; they are all good.'" The passage Johnson quoted to Reynolds is printed in *Reliquiae Baxterianae* (1696): "And yet I did usually put in something in my sermon which was above their own discovery and which they had not known before. And this I did that they might be kept humble and still perceive their ignorance and be willing to keep in a learning state. (For when preachers tell their people of no more than they know, and do not show that they excel them in knowledge and easily overtop them in abilities, the people will be tempted to turn preachers themselves, and think that they have learnt all that the ministers can teach them, and are as wise as they. . . .) And I did this also to increase their knowledge; and also to make religion pleasant to them by a daily addition to their former light, and to draw them on with desire and delight."

[2] Among the Boswell Papers is the following note in Sir Joshua's hand: ". . . Sir J. Reynolds had a note in his possession written by Pope, wherein he says that he had recommended the author of *London a Poem* to Lord Gower to be preceptor to his son, merely on account of the excellence of that poem, but without success—that he had been informed he was troubled with convulsions that made him at times a hideous spectacle. Sir Joshua informed Dr. Johnson of this note which he had in his possession, but always avoided showing it to him on account of the last words. As he often inquired after it, Sir Joshua observed to him that he seemed to be much flattered with Mr. Pope's attention

his attention was recovered. Sometimes, indeed, it would be near a minute before he would give an answer, looking as if he laboured to bring his mind to bear on the question.

The drawback to his character is entertaining prejudices on very slight foundation, giving an opinion perhaps first at random, but from its being contradicted he thinks himself obliged always stubbornly to support—or if he could not support, still not to acquiesce. Of this I remember an instance of a defect or forgetfulness in his *Dictionary*. I asked him how he came not to correct it in the second edition. "No," says he, "they made so much of it that I would not flatter them by altering it." [1] He sometimes, it must be confessed, covered his ignorance in generals, rather than appear ignorant or to be conquered in argument, [of] which he never would suffer even the appearance.

He would sometimes risk an opinion expressed in the strongest terms [on a book in] which [he] had read only a few lines. When afterwards he was forced to read it with greater attention in order to give an account of it as a critic, he thought

---

to him. 'Who', says he, 'would not be flattered with the solicitous inquiry of such a man as Pope?' Mr. Richardson told Sir Joshua that Pope had earnestly desired him to inquire who was the author, and that when he informed him that his name was Johnson, an obscure man, Mr. Pope answered, 'He will soon be *déterré*.' The event has fully justified the prediction." Boswell made use of this information in the *Life*.

[1] The reference is probably to the word *pastern*. In the summer of 1762 Johnson accompanied Reynolds to Devonshire. One day, according to Frances Reynolds, his hostess "before a large company at dinner addressed herself to him with a very audible voice, 'Pray, Dr. Johnson, what made you say in your *Dictionary* that the pastern of a horse was the knee of a horse?' 'Ignorance, madam, ignorance,' answered Johnson.'' (Boswell's version is "Ignorance, madam, pure ignorance.")

it right still to adhere to his first accidental opinion and to use all his skill in vindicating that opinion, which was not difficult for him to do. When he had made up his mind, he was firm. This was the fate of the poems of Gray,[1] and in order to depreciate them, the method he seems to have taken is to take up those higher excellencies which are on the verge of defects and condemning them as such. Thus in morality it is easy to call a generous man a spendthrift that is ignorant of the value of money, a frugal man a miser with[out] a spark of generosity, a gay character an empty fop, and a grave one a stupid blockhead. It is always to be remembered that I am giving a portrait, not a panegyric, of Dr. Johnson.

In arguing he did not trouble himself with much circumlocution, but directly and abruptly opposed his antagonist's opinion in an abrupt manner that was offensive to those who were not used to his manner. He fought with all sorts of weapons, by ludicrous comparisons and similes; if all failed, with rudeness overbearing.[2] His expressions of approbation or

[1] Johnson's formal criticism of Gray's poetry was not published until 1781. In 1763 he had said to Boswell: "Sir, I do not think Mr. Gray a superior sort of poet. He has not a bold imagination, nor much command of words. The obscurity in which he has involved himself will not make us think him sublime. His *Elegy in a Churchyard* has a happy selection of images, but I don't like his great things." In 1775, when Boswell said "Surely he was not dull in poetry," Johnson replied, "Sir, he was dull in company, dull in his closet, dull everywhere. He was dull in a new way, and that made many people think him GREAT. He was a mechanical poet."

[2] Boswell supplies the best example: "He was vehement against old Dr. Mounsey, of Chelsea College, as 'a fellow who swore and talked bawdy'. 'I have been often in his company (said Dr. Percy), and never heard him swear or talk bawdy.' Mr. Davies, who sat next to Dr. Percy, having after this had some conversation aside with him, made a discovery which, in his zeal to pay court to Dr. Johnson, he eagerly proclaimed aloud from the foot of the table: 'O, Sir, I

dislike were measured with the greatest passion, and it was seldom pleasing at the minute. He thought it necessary never to be worsted in argument, though this disposition he frequently spoke of as very weak; "as if," says he, "the character depended on one evening." He thus seemed to be schooling himself, but he never learned the thing. You will wonder to hear a person who loved him so sincerely speak thus freely of his friend, but you must recollect I am not writing his panegyric, but as if upon oath not only to give the truth but the whole truth.

From passion, from the prevalence of his disposition for

---

have found out a very good reason why Dr. Percy never heard Mounsey swear or talk bawdy; for he tells me, he never saw him but at the Duke of Northumberland's table.' 'And so, Sir (said Johnson loudly, to Dr. Percy), you would shield this man from the charge of swearing and talking bawdy because he did not do so at the Duke of Northumberland's table. Sir, you might as well tell us that you had seen him hold up his hand at the Old Bailey and he neither swore nor talked bawdy; or that you had seen him in the cart at Tyburn and he neither swore nor talked bawdy. And is it thus, Sir, that you presume to controvert what I have related?' Dr. Johnson's animadversion was uttered in such a manner that Dr. Percy seemed to be displeased and soon afterwards left the company, of which Johnson did not at that time take any notice.

"Swift having been mentioned, Johnson, as usual, treated him with little respect as an author. Some of us endeavoured to support the Dean of St. Patrick's by various arguments. One in particular praised his *Conduct of the Allies*. JOHNSON. 'Sir, his *Conduct of the Allies* is a performance of very little ability.' 'Surely, Sir (said Dr. Douglas), you must allow it has strong facts.' JOHNSON. 'Why yes, Sir; but what is that to the merit of the composition? In the Sessions-paper of the Old Bailey there are strong facts. Housebreaking is a strong fact. Robbery is a strong fact; and murder is a *mighty* strong fact. But is great praise due to the historian of those strong facts? No, Sir. Swift has told what he had to tell distinctly enough, but that is all. He had to count ten, and he has counted it right.' Then recollecting that Mr. Davies by acting as an *informer* had been the occasion of his talking somewhat too harshly to his friend Dr. Percy, for which, probably, when the first ebullition was over, he felt some compunction, he took an opportunity to give him a hit; so added, with a preparatory laugh, 'Why, Sir, Tom Davies might have written the *Conduct of the Allies*.' "

the minute, he was continually acting contrary to his reason, to his own principles. It was a frequent subject of animadversion with him, how much authors lost of the pleasure and comfort of life by their carrying always about them their own consequence and celebrity. Yet no man in mixed company—not to his intimates, certainly, for that would be an insupportable slavery—ever acted with more circumspection to his character than himself. The most light and airy dispute was with him a dispute on the Arena. He fought upon every occasion as if his whole reputation depended upon the victory of the minute, and he fought with all the weapons. If he was foiled in argument, he had recourse to abuse and rudeness. That he was not thus strenuous for victory with his intimates in *tête-á-tête* conversations, where there were no witnesses, may be easily believed. Indeed, had his conduct been to them the same as he exhibited to the public, his friends could never have entertained that love and affection for him which they all feel and profess for his memory.

But what appears extraordinary is that a man who so well saw, himself, the folly of this ambition of shining, of speaking or acting always according to the character you imagined you possessed in the world, should produce in himself the greatest example of a contrary conduct.

Were I to write the life of Dr. Johnson, I would labour this point, to separate his conduct that proceeded from his passions, and what proceeded from his reason, from his natural disposition seen in his quiet hours.

He had one virtue which I hold one of the most difficult

to practise. After the heat of contest was over, if he had been informed that his antagonist resented his rudeness, he was the first to seek after a reconciliation.[1] He took the first opportunity of addressing himself to him in a kind manner; if it was returned, he thought himself acquitted of making any humiliating [apology]. [To them that loved him not] as rough as winter; to those who sought his love as mild as summer.[2] Many instances will readily occur to those who knew him intimately of the guard which he endeavoured always to keep over himself.

The Christian religion was with him such a certain and established truth that he considered it as a kind of profanation to hold any argument about its truth.

He was not easily imposed upon by pretensions to honesty

[1] "I shall never forget," wrote Frances Reynolds, "with what regret he spoke of the rude reply he made to a reverend divine, a dignitary of the church [Dr. Barnard, Dean of Derry], on his saying that men never improved after the age of forty-five. 'That is not true, Sir,' said Johnson. 'You, who perhaps are forty-eight, may still improve if you will try. I wish you would set about it; and I am afraid,' he added, 'there is great room for it.' And this was said in rather a large party of gentlemen and ladies at dinner. Soon after the ladies withdrew from the table, Dr. Johnson followed them, and, sitting down by the lady of the house, he said, 'I am very sorry for having spoken so rudely to the [Dean].' 'You very well may, Sir.' 'Yes', he said, 'it was highly improper to speak in that style to a minister of the Gospel, and I am the more hurt on reflecting with what mild dignity he received it.' When the [Dean] came up into the drawing-room, Dr. Johnson immediately rose from his seat, and made him sit on the sofa by him, and with such a beseeching look for pardon and with such fond gestures—literally smoothing down his arms and his knees—tokens of penitence, which were so graciously received by the [Dean] as to make Dr. Johnson very happy and not a little added to the esteem and respect he had previously entertained for his character."

[2] Lofty and sour to them, that lov'd him not,
But to those men, that sought him, sweet as summer.
Henry VIII, IV. ii.

and candour, but he appeared to have little suspicion of hypocrisy in religion.

His pride had no meanness in it. There was nothing little or mean about him. His passions were like those of other men; the difference only lay in his keeping a stricter watch over himself. In petty circumstances this wayward disposition appeared, but in greater things in which he thought it worth while to summons his recollection, he came on his guard and always expressed himself as he ought. Whatever he had felt and where [he had] more time, he was certain to be right, as when he writ.

His writings and his conduct in life were employed in the promoting, to the utmost of his power, virtue and piety. As in his writings not a line can be found which a saint could wish to blot, so in his life he would never suffer the least immorality, indecency, or any conversation contrary to virtue [or] piety to proceed without a severe check, which no elevation of rank exempted them from. Such a reverence for truth [did he have] that he never infringed on it even in the slightest matter. From his reverence to truth he measured out his approbation or dislike.

Truth, whether in great or little matters, he held sacred. "From the violation of truth," he said, "in great things your character or your interest was affected; in lesser things your pleasure is equally destroyed." I remember, on his relating some incident, I added something to his relation which I supposed might likewise have happened. "It would have been a better story," says he, "if it had been so, but it was not."

Our friend Dr. Goldsmith was not so scrupulous, but he said he only indulged himself in white lies, light as feathers, which he threw up in the air, and on whomever they fell, nobody was hurt. "I wish," says Dr. Johnson, "you would take the trouble of moulting your feathers."

As an instance of refined conduct, which none [but] a man of perfect integrity could [have exhibited], I once inadvertently put him in a situation from which it would be difficult for any man to extricate himself to his own satisfaction. I pointed at some lines in *The Traveller* which I told him I was sure he writ. He hesitated a little. During this hesitation I recollected myself that, as I knew he would not lie, I put him in a cleft stick, and should have had but my due if he had given me a rough answer. But he only said, "Sir, I did write them, but that you may not imagine that I have wrote more than I really have, the utmost that I have wrote in that poem, to the best of my recollection, is not more than eighteen lines." It must be observed there was then an opinion about town that Dr. Johnson wrote the whole poem for his friend, who was then in a manner an unknown writer.

This conduct appears to me to be in the highest degree correct and refined. If the doctor's conscience would have let him told a lie, the matter would have been soon over. If it had not even been of a very refined nature, he might have satisfied it by giving no answer, however conscious he would be that silence in this case would be here all the eloquence that was required effectually to discover the truth. It would be telling it in words; and, as I said, to a pretty gross conscience his secrecy would have moulted never a feather, and though an additional falsehood, it would have been inferred that he had writ the whole. All this by the just conduct of Dr. Johnson was prevented.

Custom, or politeness, or courtly manners has authorised such an Eastern hyperbolical style of compliment that part of Dr. Johnson's character for rudeness of manners must be put to the account of this scrupulous adherence to truth. His obstinate silence, whilst all the company were in raptures, vying with each other who should pepper highest,[1] was considered as rudeness or ill-nature.

This caution appears to be necessary to a biographer, supposing the biography to consist in anecdotes, as in Dr. Johnson's case:—to proportion the eccentric parts of his character to the proportion of his book. A short book containing an account of all the peculiarities or absurdities of a man would leave on the reader's mind an impression of an absurd character. That Johnson was rude at times cannot be denied, but by reading any account of him you would shrink at the idea of being in his company. Every prominent part of a man's character, every eccentric action when exerted, counts for ten, like some particular cards in games. Ten negatives amount to one affirmation. I know no greater inducement to uniform propriety of conduct than this consideration: how much one breach of uniformity cancels a great number of acts of a regular and conformable consistency.

[1] Compare Goldsmith's lines on Garrick, below, p. 83. The text of this paragraph is taken from Leslie's version, because the original is not now with the rest of the manuscript.

The prejudices he had to countries did not extend to individuals. The chief prejudice in which he indulged himself was against Scotland, though he had the most cordial friendship with individuals [of that country]. This he used to vindicate as a duty. In respect to Frenchmen he rather laughed at himself; but it was unsurmountable that he considered every foreigner as a fool till they had convinced him of the contrary.[1] Against the Irish he entertained no prejudice. He thought they united themselves very well with us, but whilst the Scotch when in England united and made a party by employing only Scotch servants and Scotch tradesmen, he held it right for Englishmen to oppose a party against them.[2]

This reasoning would have more weight if the numbers were equal. A small body in a larger has such general disadvantages that I fear are scarce counterbalanced by whatever little combination they can make. A general combination against them would be too much and would be little short of annihilation.

In his last minutes he received great comfort from the recollection that he hoped he had endeavoured to promote the cause of virtue. During his last illness, when all hope was at an end, he appeared to be quieter and more resigned. His approaching dissolution was always present to his mind. A few days before he died, Mr. Langton and myself only present, he

[1] "His unjust contempt for foreigners," wrote Langton, "was indeed extreme. One evening, at Old Slaughter's coffee-house, when a number of them were talking loud about little matters, he said, 'Does not this confirm old Meynell's observation—*For any thing I see, foreigners are fools.*' "

[2] "Talking of the success of the Scotch in London," reports Boswell, "he imputed it in a considerable degree to their spirit of nationality. 'You know, Sir (said he), that no Scotchman publishes a book or has a play brought upon the stage but there are five hundred people ready to applaud him.' "

said he had been a great sinner, but he hoped he had given no bad example by his writing nor to his friends; that he had some consolation in reflecting that he had never denied Christ, and repeated the text "whoever denies me", &c. We were both very ready to assure him that we were conscious that we were better and wiser from his life and conversation, and that, so far from denying Christ, he had been in this age his greatest champion.[1]

Sometimes a flash of wit escaped him as if involuntary. He was asked how he liked the new man that was hired to watch by him. "Instead of watching," says he, "he sleeps like a dormouse; and when he helps me to bed he is as awkward as a turnspit dog the first time he is put into the wheel."

Dr. Johnson might justly, as in reality he did, console himself a few days before his death with the hope that he had given neither by his writings or his conduct a bad example to mankind or to his friends. In no respect could the advantage of the practice of truth be more clearly demonstrated than by his own conduct and habits. The confidence which his friends reposed in his veracity and the satisfaction and pleasure which they consequently experienced from everything he told them could not fail to incite them to imitate a quality which increased so much the pleasure of society, the love and confidence of friends, and the increase of their own honour.

[1] Langton and Reynolds were alone with Johnson on 29 November, when, according to Langton, Johnson's "hopes were increased, and . . . he was much cheered upon being reminded of the general tendency of his writings and of his example". For the text Johnson repeated, *see* Matt. 10. 33.

V

GARRICK AND REYNOLDS

WITH the contemporary verdict on Garrick's skill as an actor Sir Joshua was in agreement. Furthermore he believed that unlike most actors Garrick was also a good judge of plays. But he was well aware of Garrick's faults, as this brief but striking character sketch makes evident.

The manuscript, which turned up at Malahide Castle with the Goldsmith memoir, gives no clue as to when or why it was written, but it is clear that when writing it Reynolds was remembering the many conversations which he had had with friends about the great actor. In particular he here echoes what was said at Topham Beauclerk's in the spring of 1779, three months after Garrick's death. Boswell's version follows: "On Saturday, April 24, I dined with [Johnson] at Mr. Beauclerk's with Sir Joshua Reynolds, Mr. Jones (afterwards Sir William), Mr. Langton, Mr. Steevens, Mr. Paradise, and Dr. Higgins. I mentioned that Mr. Wilkes had attacked Garrick to me, as a man who had no friend. JOHNSON: 'I believe he is right, Sir. *Ὦι φίλοι, οὐ φίλος*—He had friends, but no friend. Garrick was so diffused, he had no man to whom he wished to unbosom himself. He found people always ready to applaud him, and that always for the same thing, so he saw life with great uniformity.' I took upon me, for once, to fight with Goliath's weapons, and play the sophist. 'Garrick did not need a friend, as he got from everybody all he wanted. What is a friend? One who supports you and comforts you, while others do not. Friendship, you know, Sir, is the cordial drop, "to make the nauseous draught of life go down," but if the draught be not nauseous, if it be all sweet, there is no occasion for that drop.' JOHNSON: 'Many men would not be content to live so. I hope I should not. They would wish to have an intimate friend, with whom they might compare minds and cherish private virtues.' One of the company mentioned Lord Chesterfield as a man who had no friend. JOHNSON: 'There were more materials to make friendship in Garrick, had he not been so diffused.' BOSWELL: 'Garrick was pure gold, but beat out to thin leaf. Lord Chesterfield was tinsel.' JOHNSON: 'Garrick was a very good man, the cheerfullest man of his age; a decent liver in a profession which is supposed to give indulgence to licentiousness, and a man who gave away, freely, money acquired by himself.' "

The remarks just quoted serve in part to explain why Reynolds did not have for Garrick the feelings he had for Goldsmith and Johnson. Sir Joshua liked men who would relax when among friends; he enjoyed those who would "unbosom" themselves at the proper time. He disliked Garrick's artificiality, his vanity.

The two must have met at about the time Reynolds met Johnson—in the middle '50s. In a commonplace-book kept at about this time Reynolds records his admiration of Garrick's critical powers. The first of many portraits was probably begun in 1759 and thereafter the actor was frequently in his studio. Reynolds was an ardent theatre-goer, admired Garrick's acting, was amused at his sprightliness. But as a man he held him in something approximating contempt. Here is a story which Sir Joshua told Malone.

"Not long before Garrick's death, he invited Charles Fox, Mr. Burke, Mr. Gibbon, Mr. Sheridan, Sir Joshua Reynolds, Mr. Beauclerk, and some others to dine at Hampton. Soon after dinner he began to read a copy of verses, written by himself on some of the most celebrated men of the time, including two or three of those who were present. They were not very well satisfied with their characters, and still less when describing Lord Thurlow, who was not present, he introduced the words, '*superior parts.*' Mr. Burke, speaking of his own character, said afterwards to Sir Joshua Reynolds, that he was almost ready to have spat in his face.

"Garrick, finding the company uncommonly grave, in consequence of his unlucky verses, before they had drunk half a dozen glasses of wine proposed to adjourn to his lawn, where they would find some amusement. When there, the whole amusement con-

DAVID GARRICK, BY REYNOLDS

"Garrick between Tragedy and Comedy. The former exhorts him to follow her exalted vocation, but Comedy drags him away, and he seems to yield willingly, though endeavouring to excuse himself, and pleading that he is forced. Tragedy is a good antique figure, but wants more dignity in the expression of her face. Comedy is a beautiful and winning girl—but Garrick's face is distorted and burlesque."—HORACE WALPOLE

sisted in an old man and a young one running backwards and forwards between two baskets filled with stones, and whoever emptied his basket first was to be the victor. Garrick expected that his guests would have been interested and have betted on the runners; but between ill humour with his verses and being dragged from table the instant dinner had been finished, no interest whatever was expressed in what, from the anticipations of their host, so much had been expected. All was cold and spiritless—one of the most vapid days they had ever spent. If Garrick had not laid these plots for merriment, but let conversation take its common course, all would have gone well. Such men as I have mentioned could not have passed a dull day."

Sir Joshua's account of Garrick is not balanced as are the sketches he drew of Goldsmith and Johnson. It is a hostile account. But what he has to say is verified by the comments of many of his contemporaries. In a sense what Reynolds has done is to write a prose version of Goldsmith's brilliant characterisation in *Retaliation*.

> On the stage he was natural, simple, affecting;
> 'Twas only that when he was off, he was acting.

This in turn echoes a *bon mot* which the actor-dramatist Samuel Foote was said to have originated. "Foote being at supper one night at the Bedford coffee-house just after Garrick had performed Macbeth, the conversation very naturally turned on the merits of that great performer, when after many eulogiums of the universality of his powers, it was given up to him to be the first actor on any stage. 'By G—d, gentlemen,' says Foote, 'I do not think you have above half said enough of him, for I think him not only the greatest actor on, but off the stage.' "

Again, when Sir Joshua speaks of the sycophants catering to Garrick's love of flattery, he seems to be paraphrasing Goldsmith:

> Of praise a mere glutton, he swallowed what came;
> And the puff of a dunce, he mistook it for fame;
> 'Till his relish grown callous, almost to disease,
> Who peppered the highest was surest to please.

To illustrate this foible one anecdote should suffice. At the height of his fame Garrick, while sitting for his bust to Nollekens the sculptor, asked with assumed casualness what people were saying about him. "Indeed," replied Nollekens gravely, "I heard somebody speaking very highly in your praise, as high as possible." Garrick quickly asked, "Pray who was it—who was it spoke so highly in my praise?" "Why," replied Nollekens, "it was yourself"—a remark which the sitter considered "damned vulgar".

Once when Northcote was a pupil living in Sir Joshua's house he "heard Garrick complain that it was a very great fatigue to him to dine in company so frequently as his interest seemed to require. From hence we may conclude, that he considered himself as under the necessity of being a very delightful companion, which he certainly was; but had he been content to be like other persons at table, it would have then been no fatigue to him. On the same account he avoided ever going to a masquerade in any specific personification, as that would have involved him in the difficulty of supporting his character as a wit."

In his commonplace-book Malone writes to the same effect: "Mr. Garrick always took care to leave company with a good impression in his favour. After he had told some good story or defeated an antagonist by wit or raillery, he often disappointed people who hoped that he would continue to entertain them and receive the praise and admiration they were ready enough to give. But he was so artificial that he could break away in the midst of the highest festivity, merely in order to secure the impression he had made. On this part of his character it was well said by Colman that he never came into company without laying a plot for an escape out of it."

Percy Fitzgerald in his *Life of Garrick* asserts that Sir Joshua "bears testimony to the charm of [Garrick's] company at the great tables, his gaiety, subdued vivacity, his wit on light subjects, and his acuteness and information in graver matters." Sir Joshua does nothing of the sort. Fitzgerald, of course, knew nothing of the character sketch which is here first printed and wove his fiction from materials found in the Johnsonian dialogues which are reprinted in this book. That the memoir rather than the dialogues represents Sir Joshua's real opinion of Garrick is indisputable. The germ of it is a note in the Boswell Papers, which Sir Joshua made while Garrick was alive.

> Gar. by too great a desire after the reputation of being a wit, the object from whom the whole company are to receive their entertainment, spoils every company he goes into.

Apparently the sketch was never completed. What has survived is an extremely rough draft in which the author has tried various ways of phrasing his ideas. The text here established includes some phrases which were deleted, excludes some which were substituted, the aim being to present what in the editor's opinion is the most intelligible account. The last paragraph in particular lacks the polish which is seen in what Sir Joshua allowed himself to send to a printer. But though the manuscript is a crude one, it is none the less interesting, supplementing as it does the portraits of the actor which Reynolds handed down to posterity.

REYNOLDS ON GARRICK

Garrick from his early youth, when he used to repeat passages in plays and act whole parts in private theatres, naturally imbibed a desire for popular applause. Afterwards, when he entered the great world and had enlarged his circle, this universal passion was not likely to be much abated; 'twas the employment of his mind, night and day, by what means he could improve and advance his reputation. His profession of an actor he studied with the greatest attention. He left nothing to chance. Every attitude, however it might have the appearance of immediate impulse, was the result of various trials in his closet.

Great as Garrick was on the stage, he was at least equal if not still superior at the table, and here he had too much the same habit of preparing himself, as if he was to act a principal part.

The man himself is not likely to be the last who discovers his own excellence. Garrick knew it and made himself a slave to his reputation. Amongst the variety of arts observed by his friends to preserve that reputation, one of them was to make himself rare. It was difficult to get him and when you had him, as difficult to keep him. He never came into company but with a plot how to get out of it. He was for ever receiving messages of his being wanted in another place. It was a rule with him

DAVID GARRICK, BY REYNOLDS

"A fine head of Garrick by Sir Joshua, painted for Mrs. Thrale, and the last portrait of that great actor done by Reynolds."—NORTHCOTE

never to leave any company saturated. Being used to exhibit himself at a theatre or a large table, he did not consider an individual as worth powder and shot.

The habit of seeking fame in this manner left his mind unfit for the cultivation of private friendship. Garrick died without a real friend, though no man had a greater number of what the world calls friends. Garrick had no friends to whom he gave orders that he was always at home, except to his doctors, of which he had two sorts, one sort administering for his body, the other for his diseased mind—in other words, his vanity. The first were generally quacks and the others sycophants.

Garrick, as I observed, died without a friend; so did Lord Chesterfield. The moral to be drawn from their lives is this: that this passion for fame, however proper when within due bounds as a link in the social chain, as a spur to our exertions to acquire and deserve the affections of our brethren, yet when this passion is carried to excess, like every other excess it becomes a vice, either ridiculous, or odious, or sometimes criminal. An inordinate desire after fame produces an entire neglect of their old friends, or we may rather say they never have any friends; their whole desire and ambition is centred in extending their reputation by showing their tricks before fresh new men. That moment you begin to congratulate yourself on your new acquaintance, your intimacy ceases. A worse consequence: by degrees all the principles of right and wrong, whatever dignifies human nature, is lost, or not attended to when in competition with the shadow of fame. They begin to grow short-sighted and seize with such greediness the immediate gratification that they forfeit every title to what is truly praiseworthy, steadiness of conduct. From having no great general principle they live in perpetual anxiety what conduct to take on every occasion to insure this petty praise.

VI

SIR JOSHUA'S TWO DIALOGUES

ILLUSTRATING JOHNSON'S MANNER OF CONVERSATION

IN the spring of 1831 the wit and politician Joseph Jekyll sent a pamphlet to his scholarly friend George Agar Ellis, accompanied by the following note: "This unpublished squib of the late Sir Joshua Reynolds was given to me some short time ago by his only surviving niece, and I lent it to Croker for his five forthcoming volumes of Dr. Johnson. As it is scarce you may like to look at it." The pamphlet was entitled *Johnson and Garrick*. It had been privately printed in 1816 by Lady Thomond, the former Mary Palmer, and distributed to friends as a memorial to her uncle. She died in 1820 and was survived by her sister Mrs. Gwatkin.

Croker reprinted the pamphlet as an appendix to his fourth volume, giving credit not to Jekyll but to Mrs. Gwyn, *née* Horneck. He adds that Sir Joshua himself had given a copy of it to Sir George Beaumont. This copy would necessarily have been in manuscript—and may still be in existence. The only known manuscript, now in the Yale University Library, is the one used by the printers in 1816. It is in the hand of Mary Palmer, who spent much of her time towards the end of her uncle's life in making fair copies of what he was writing. Reynolds himself has corrected her copy in some places.[1]

Croker was not the first to reprint the dialogues. They appeared in the *London New Monthly Magazine* for August, 1816, and again in November of that year in the *North American Review*. A few years

[1] As the illustration makes clear, the first page of the manuscript is inaccurately headed "Johnson in favour of Garrick". The printed version read properly "Johnson against Garrick".

later Laetitia Matilda Hawkins, daughter of Sir John, was compiling her memoirs and received permission to include them in her book. She introduces them with an elaborate sentence, calculated to deceive no one who belonged to the initiated: "A lady whose uncle was one of Johnson's friends, and who lived in great intimacy with Sir Joshua Reynolds's family, has allowed me to print the following *jeu d'esprit*, which in my humble judgment is a very vivid imitation of Johnson's language and manner." Croker seems to be the only person on record who does not agree with Miss Hawkins in praising the piece. He considered it "faint, one might almost say feeble", when compared to the conversations recorded by Boswell.

Boswell's journal supplies the only contemporary reference to the dialogues. On 9 September 1790, he played whist at Sir Joshua's, and after supper the host "entertained Dr. Lawrence and Malone and me with a dialogue which he had composed between himself and Dr. Johnson." Since Boswell refers to *a* dialogue between Reynolds and Johnson, it is possible that the companion piece had not yet been written. In any event the reference tends to prove that the dialogues were written at the close of Sir Joshua's life. This was the period when the proof-sheets of the *Life* were being sent to Sir Joshua's home, where Boswell read them aloud. Reynolds had been forced to give up painting because of his failing eyesight. He had little to occupy his time. As he heard Boswell's vivid descriptions of Johnson talking for victory, he must have determined to try his hand at writing several scenes which would show in an amusing way why Johnson's friends enjoyed listening to him.

The two dialogues, as has often been said, were written to illustrate a remark of Sir Joshua's which Boswell quotes, "that Johnson considered Garrick to be as it were his *property*. He would allow no man either to blame or to praise Garrick in his presence, without contradicting him." But Reynolds is at the same time illustrating the way in which Johnson was managed by his friends.

Note that at the beginning Sir Joshua says in an aside that he will "bring him out". It is a reminder to us that Johnson had to be stirred up before he would talk. He was, to repeat Tyers's apt

Johnson in favour of Garrick 1

R. Let me alone, I'll bring him out — (aside

— I have been thinking Dr Johnson this morning on a matter that has puzzled me very much, it is a subject that I dare say has often pass'd in your thoughts, & tho' I cannot, I dare say you have made up your mind upon it.

J. Tilly fally, what is all this preparation what is all this mighty matter?

Rey. Why, it is a very weighty matter. The subject I have been thinking upon is, predestination & free will, two things I cannot reconcile together for the life of me in my opinion Dr Johnson Free will & foreknowledge cannot be reconciled.

FIRST PAGE OF THE DIALOGUES, CHIEFLY IN THE HAND OF MARY PALMER

"Dear Sir Joshua, even with his inimitable pencil, never drew more interesting, more resembling portraits [than in these dialogues]. I hear them all speak. I see every action, every gesture which accompanied every word. I hear the deep-toned and indignant accents of our friend Johnson; I hear the affected periods of Gibbon; the natural, the easy, the friendly, the elegant language, the polished sarcasm, softened with the sweet temper, of Sir Joshua."—HANNAH MORE

statement, like a ghost, who would not speak until spoken to. In the first dialogue, then, Reynolds is deliberately goading his friend. In other words, he is asking for the rudeness which he receives. Perhaps the nicest of the nice touches in the dialogue is Johnson's charge that Reynolds is rude—this coming after Johnson's repeated interruptions and his pointed allusion to Sir Joshua's deafness.

Reynolds "was wise enough", writes R. Brimley Johnson, "to see that it was the dictator's abuse of his friends one should discount, not his generous praise. He has given us the real Johnson by producing three pages 'against', and ten 'for', David Garrick: a very proper proportion to represent the real nature of the man." Perhaps this is true. The over-all impression which the dialogues make on the reader is favourable to Garrick and thus, in a sense, to Johnson. And the choice of the cynical, sceptical Gibbon as the attacker of Garrick is a happy one. But it should be noted that at the end of the second dialogue Johnson has been manœuvred into attacking Garrick once more. When Gibbon maintains that the actor felt passion at the moment he represented it, Johnson replies: "About as much as Punch feels. That Garrick himself gave in to this foppery of feelings I can easily believe; but he knew at the same time that he lied." And we are back to the starting point once more.

The danger in making statements like R. Brimley Johnson's is that they may encourage us to take a further step and use the dialogues to prove what Reynolds thought of Garrick. This, as has been earlier said, was done by Percy Fitzgerald, who asserts that what Reynolds really thought about Garrick he has put in Johnson's mouth in the second dialogue. To know what Reynolds really thought we must not turn to dramatic writing. When composing these dialogues Reynolds was aiming to amuse and was concentrating on how Johnson behaved in society. The dialogues, written in a light and bantering fashion, are the more delightful when read immediately after Sir Joshua's memoir of Garrick.

JOHNSON AGAINST GARRICK

REYNOLDS. Let me alone, I'll bring him out. (*Aside.*)—I have been thinking, Dr. Johnson, this morning, on a matter that has puzzled me very much. It is a subject that I dare say has often passed in your thoughts, and though *I* cannot, I dare say *you* have made up your mind upon it.

JOHNSON. Tilly fally![1] What is all this preparation, what is all this mighty matter?

REYNOLDS. Why, it is a very weighty matter. The subject I have been thinking upon is predestination and free will, two things I cannot reconcile together for the life of me. In my opinion, Dr. Johnson, free will and foreknowledge cannot be reconciled.

JOHNSON. Sir, it is not of very great importance what your opinion is upon such a question.

REYNOLDS. But I meant only, Dr. Johnson, to know your opinion.

JOHNSON. No, Sir, you meant no such thing; you meant only to show these gentlemen that you are not the man they took you to be, but that you think of high matters sometimes, and that you may have the credit of having it said that you held an argument with Sam Johnson on predestination and free will; a subject of that magnitude as to have engaged the attention of the world, to have perplexed the wisdom of man for these two

[1] "Nonsense!"—a phrase common in the sixteenth century.

thousand years; a subject on which the fallen angels, who *had yet not lost all their original brightness*, find themselves *in wandering mazes lost*.[1] That such a subject could be discussed in the levity of convivial conversation, is a degree of absurdity beyond what is easily conceivable.

REYNOLDS. It is so, as you say; to be sure. I talked once to our friend Garrick upon this subject, but I remember we could make nothing of it.

JOHNSON. O noble pair!

REYNOLDS. Garrick was a clever fellow, Dr. Johnson. Garrick, take him altogether, was certainly a very great man.

JOHNSON. Garrick, Sir, may be a great man in your opinion, as far as I know. But he was not so in mine. Little things are great to little men.[2]

REYNOLDS. I have heard you say, Dr. Johnson—

JOHNSON. Sir, you never heard me say that David Garrick was a great man. You may have heard me say that Garrick was a good repeater—of other men's words—words put into his mouth by other men. This makes but a faint approach towards being a great man.

REYNOLDS. But take Garrick upon the whole. Now, in regard to conversation—

JOHNSON. Well, Sir, in regard to conversation, I never discovered in the conversation of David Garrick any intellectual energy, any wide grasp of thought, any extensive comprehension

[1] The phrases in italics are from *Paradise Lost*, I. 591 and II. 561.

[2] A line from Goldsmith's *Traveller*, often quoted by Johnson:

These little things are great to little man.

of mind, or that he possessed any of those powers to which *great* could, with any degree of propriety, be applied.

REYNOLDS. But still—

JOHNSON. Hold, Sir, I have not done. There are, to be sure, in the laxity of colloquial speech, various kinds of greatness. A man may be a great tobacconist, a man may be a great painter, he may be likewise a great mimic. Now you may be the one and Garrick the other, and yet neither of you be great men.

REYNOLDS. But, Dr. Johnson—

JOHNSON. Hold, Sir. I have often lamented how dangerous it is to investigate and to discriminate character, to men who have no discriminative powers.

REYNOLDS. But Garrick, as a companion, I heard you say—no longer ago than last Wednesday, at Mr. Thrale's table—

JOHNSON. You tease me, Sir. Whatever you may have heard me say—no longer ago than last Wednesday, at Mr. Thrale's table—I tell you I do not say so now. Besides, as I said before, you may not have understood me; you misapprehended me; you may not have heard me.

REYNOLDS. I am very sure I heard you.

JOHNSON. Besides, besides, Sir, besides,—do you not know—are you so ignorant as not to know—that it is the highest degree of rudeness to quote a man against himself?

REYNOLDS. But if you differ from yourself, and give one opinion today—

JOHNSON. Have done, Sir. The company, you see, are tired, as well as myself.

T'OTHER SIDE

JOHNSON. No, Sir.[1] Garrick's fame was prodigious, not only in England but over all Europe. Even in Russia I have been told he was a proverb; when any one had repeated well, he was called a second Garrick.

GIBBON. I think he had full as much reputation as he deserved.

JOHNSON. I do not pretend to know, Sir, what your meaning may be by saying he had as much reputation as he deserved. He deserved much, and he had much.

GIBBON. Why, surely, Dr. Johnson, his merit was in small things only. He had none of those qualities that make a real great man.

JOHNSON. Sir, I as little understand what your meaning may be when you speak of the qualities that make a great man. It is a vague term. Garrick was no common man. A man above the common size of men may surely, without any great impropriety, be called a great man. In my opinion he has very reasonably fulfilled the prophecy which he once reminded me of having made to his mother: when she asked me how little

[1] Boswell noted that Johnson's "frequent use of the expression, *No, Sir*, was not always to intimate contradiction; for he would say so when he was about to enforce an affirmative proposition which had not been denied. . . . I used to consider it as a kind of flag of defiance; as if he had said, 'Any argument you may offer against this, is not just. No, Sir, it is not.' It was like Falstaff's 'I deny your major.' "

David went on at school, that I should say to her[1] that he would come to be hanged or come to be a great man. No, Sir, it is undoubtedly true that the same qualities, united with virtue or with vice, make a hero or a rogue, a great general or a great highwayman. Now Garrick, we are sure, was never hanged, and in regard to his being a great man, you must take the whole man together. It must be considered in how many things Garrick excelled in which every man desires to excel. Setting aside his excellence as an actor, in which he is acknowledged to be unrivalled, as a man, as a poet, as a convivial companion, you will find but few his equal and none his superior. As a man he was kind, friendly, benevolent, and generous.

GIBBON. Of Garrick's generosity I never heard. I understood his character to be totally the reverse and that he was reckoned to have loved money.

JOHNSON. That he loved money, nobody will dispute; who does not? But if you mean by loving money that he was parsimonious to a fault, Sir, you have been misinformed. To Foote and such scoundrels who circulated these reports, to such profligate spendthrifts prudence is meanness and economy is avarice. That Garrick in early youth was brought up in strict habits of economy I believe; and that they were necessary I have heard from himself. To suppose that Garrick might inadvertently act from this habit, and be saving in small things, can be no wonder. But let it be remembered at the same time that if he was frugal by habit, he was liberal from principle;

[1] The phrasing here is obscure. Probably Reynolds meant: "when she asked me how little David went on at school, I said to her that," etc. Garrick had been one of Johnson's pupils.

EDWARD GIBBON, BY REYNOLDS

"The picture . . . painted by Sir J. Reynolds and the prints made from it are as like the original as it is possible to be. When he was introduced to a blind French lady the servant happening to stretch out her mistress's hand to lay hold of the historian's cheek, she thought upon feeling its rounded contour that some trick was being played upon her with the *sitting* part of a child, and exclaimed, 'Fi donc!' "—MALONE

that when he acted from reflection, he did what his fortune enabled him to do, and what was expected from such a fortune. I remember no instance of David's parsimony but once, when he stopped Mrs. Woffington from replenishing the tea-pot; it was already, he said, as red as blood. And this instance is doubtful and happened many years ago. In the latter part of his life I observed no blamable parsimony in David. His table was elegant and even splendid. His house both in town and country, his equipage, and I think all his habits of life, were such as might be expected from a man who had acquired great riches. In regard to his generosity, which you seem to question, I shall only say there is no man to whom I would apply with more confidence of success for the loan of two hundred pounds to assist a common friend than to David; and this too with very little, if any, probability of its being repaid.

GIBBON. You were going to say something of him as a writer. You don't rate him very high as a poet.

JOHNSON. Sir, a man may be a respectable poet without being a Homer, as a man may be a good player without being a Garrick. In the lighter kinds of poetry, in the appendages of the drama, he was *if not the first, in the very first class.*[1] He had a readiness and facility, a dexterity of mind that appeared extraordinary even to men of experience, and who are not apt to wonder from ignorance. Writing prologues, epilogues, and epigrams he said he considered as his trade; and he was what a man should be, always and at all times ready at his trade. He

[1] Paraphrased from the line applied to Garrick in Goldsmith's *Retaliation*:
As a wit, if not first, in the very first line.

required two hours for a prologue or epilogue and five minutes for an epigram. Once at Burke's the company proposed a subject, and Garrick finished his epigram within the time. The same experiment was repeated in the garden, and with the same success.

GIBBON. Garrick had some flippancy of parts, to be sure, and was brisk and lively in company, and by the help of mimicry and story-telling made himself a pleasant companion. But here the whole world gave the superiority to Foote; and Garrick himself appears to have felt as if his genius was rebuked by the superior powers of Foote. It has been often observed that Garrick never dared to enter into competition with him, but was content to act an under-part to bring Foote out.

JOHNSON. That this conduct of Garrick's might be interpreted by the gross minds of Foote and his friends as if he was afraid to encounter him, I can easily imagine. Of the natural superiority of Garrick over Foote, this conduct is an instance. He disdained entering into competition with such a fellow and made him the buffoon of the company; or, as you say, brought him out. And what was at last brought out but coarse jests and vulgar merriment, indecency and impiety, a relation of events which, upon the face of them, could never have happened, characters grossly conceived and as coarsely represented? Foote was even no mimic. He went out of himself, it is true, but without going into another man. He was excelled by Garrick even in this, which is considered as Foote's greatest excellence. Garrick, besides his exact imitation of the voice and gesture of his original, to a degree of refinement of which

Foote had no conception, exhibited the mind and mode of thinking of the person imitated. Besides, Garrick confined his powers within the limits of decency. He had a character to preserve; Foote had none. By Foote's buffoonery and broad-faced merriment, private friendship, public decency, and everything estimable amongst men were trod under foot. We all know the difference of their reception in the world. No man, however high in rank or literature, but was proud to know Garrick and was glad to have him at his table. No man ever considered or treated Garrick as a player. He may be said to have stepped out of his own rank into a higher, and by raising himself he raised the rank of his profession. At a convivial table his exhilarating powers were unrivalled. He was lively, entertaining, quick in discerning the ridicule of life, and as ready in representing it; and on graver subjects there were few topics in which he could not bear his part. It is injurious to the character of Garrick to be named in the same breath with Foote. That Foote was admitted sometimes into good company (to do the man what credit I can) I will allow, but then it was merely to play tricks. Foote's merriment was that of a buffoon, and Garrick's that of a gentleman.

GIBBON. I have been told, on the contrary, that Garrick in company had not the easy manners of a gentleman.

JOHNSON. Sir, I don't know what you may have been told, or what your ideas may be of the manners of gentlemen. Garrick had no vulgarity in his manners. It is true Garrick had not the airiness of a fop, nor did he assume an affected indifference to what was passing. He did not lounge from the table to the window and from thence to the fire; or whilst you were addressing your discourse to him, turn from you and talk to his next neighbour; or give any indication that he was tired of his company. If such manners form your ideas of a fine gentleman, Garrick certainly had them not.

GIBBON. I mean that Garrick was more overawed by the presence of the great, and more obsequious to rank, than Foote, who considered himself as their equal, and treated them with the same familiarity as they treated each other.

JOHNSON. He did so, and what did the fellow get by it? The grossness of his mind prevented him from seeing that this familiarity was merely suffered, as they would play with a dog. He got no ground by affecting to call peers by their surnames. The foolish fellow fancied that lowering them was raising himself to their level. This affectation of familiarity with the great, this childish ambition of momentary exaltation obtained by the neglect of those ceremonies which custom has established as the barriers between one order of society and another, only showed his folly and meanness. He did not see that by encroaching on others' dignity, he puts himself in their power either to be repelled with helpless indignity, or endured by clemency and condescension. Garrick, by paying due respect to rank, respected himself. What he gave was returned, and what was returned he kept for ever. His advancement was on firm ground. He was recognised in public as well as respected in private. And as no man was ever more courted and better received by the public, so no man was ever less spoiled by its flattery. Garrick continued advancing to the last, till he had acquired every advantage that high birth or title could bestow, except the precedence of going into a room. But when he was there, he was treated with as much attention as the first man at the table. It is to the credit of Garrick that he never laid any claim to this distinction. It was as voluntarily allowed as if it had been his birthright. In this, I confess, I looked on David with some degree of envy, not so much for the respect he received, as for the manner of its being acquired. What fell into his lap unsought, I have been forced to claim. I began the world by fighting my way. There was something about me that invited insult, or at least a disposition to neglect; and I was equally disposed to repel insult and to claim attention, and, I fear, continue too much in this disposition now it is no longer necessary. I receive at present as much favour as I have a right to expect. I am not one of the complainers of the neglect of merit.

GIBBON. *Your* pretensions, Dr. Johnson, nobody will dispute. I cannot place Garrick on the same footing. Your reputation will continue increasing after your death, when Garrick will be totally forgot. You will be for ever considered as a classic—

JOHNSON. Enough, Sir, enough. The company would be better pleased to see us quarrel than bandying compliments.

GIBBON. But you must allow, Dr. Johnson, that Garrick was too much a slave to fame, or rather to the mean ambition of living with the great, terribly afraid of making himself cheap even with them; by which he debarred himself of much pleasant society. Employing so much attention and so much management upon such little things implies, I think, a little mind. It was observed by his friend Colman that he never went into company but with a plot how to get out of it. He was every minute called out and went off or returned as there was not a probability of his shining.

JOHNSON. In regard to his mean ambition, as you call it, of living with the great, what was the boast of Pope[1] and is every man's wish can be no reproach to Garrick. He who says he despises it knows he lies. That Garrick husbanded his fame, the fame which he had justly acquired both at the theatre and at the table, is not denied; but where is the blame, either in the one or the other, of leaving as little as he could to chance? Besides, Sir, consider what you have said. You first deny Garrick's pretensions to fame and then accuse him of too great an attention to preserve what he never possessed.

GIBBON. I don't understand—

JOHNSON. Sir, I can't help that.

GIBBON. Well, but, Dr. Johnson, you will not vindicate him in his over and above attention to his fame, his inordinate desire to exhibit himself to new men, like a coquette, ever seeking after new conquests, to the total neglect of old friends and admirers:

"He threw off his friends like a huntsman his pack,"

always looking out for new game.

JOHNSON. When you quoted the line from Goldsmith, you ought, in fairness, to have given what followed:

[1] "Envy must own, I live among the Great" (Line 133 of Pope's *First Satire of the Second Book of Horace, Imitated*).

"He knew when he pleased he could whistle them back;" which implies, at least, that he possessed a power over other men's minds approaching to fascination. But consider, Sir, what is to be done. Here is a man whom every other man desired to know. Garrick could not receive and cultivate all, according to each man's conception of his own value. We are all apt enough to consider ourselves as possessing a right to be excepted from the common crowd. Besides, Sir, I do not see why that should be imputed to him as a crime which we all so irresistibly feel and practise. We all make a greater exertion in the presence of new men than old acquaintance. It is undoubtedly true that Garrick divided his attention among so many that but little was left to the share of any individual. Like the extension and dissipation of water into dew, there was not quantity united sufficiently to quench any man's thirst. But this is the inevitable state of things. Garrick, no more than another man, could unite what, in their natures, are incompatible.

GIBBON. But Garrick not only was excluded by this means from real friendship, but accused of treating those whom he called friends with insincerity and double-dealing.

JOHNSON. Sir, it is not true. His character in that respect is misunderstood. Garrick was, to be sure, very ready in promising, but he intended at that time to fulfil his promise. He intended no deceit. His politeness or his good nature, call it which you will, made him unwilling to deny. He wanted the courage to say *no*, even to unreasonable demands. This was the great error of his life. By raising expectations which he did not

—perhaps could not—gratify, he made many enemies. At the same time it must be remembered that this error proceeded from the same cause which produced many of his virtues. Friendships, from warmth of temper too suddenly taken up and too violent to continue, ended as they were like to do, in disappointment. Enmity succeeded disappointment. His friends became his enemies; and those, having been fostered in his bosom, well knew his sensibility to reproach; and they took care that he should be amply supplied with such bitter potions as they were capable of administering. Their impotent efforts he ought to have despised, but he felt them; nor did he affect insensibility.

GIBBON. And that sensibility probably shortened his life.

JOHNSON. No, Sir. He died of a disorder of which you or any other man may die without being killed by too much sensibility.

GIBBON. But you will allow, however, that this sensibility, those fine feelings, made him the great actor he was.

JOHNSON. This is all cant, fit only for kitchen-wenches and chambermaids. Garrick's trade was to represent passion, not to feel it. Ask Reynolds whether he felt the distress of Count Ugolino[1] when he drew it.

GIBBON. But surely he feels the passion at the moment he is representing it.

[1] MS: *Hugolino*. In 1773 Reynolds had exhibited *Ugolino and his Children in the Dungeon*, the scene based on Dante's description in the thirty-third canto of the *Inferno*. There is a certain irony, presumably unintentional, in this sentence. Sir Joshua was not thinking of Ugolino when he began the picture. It was only after the central figure had been drawn that the likeness was suggested to him.

JOHNSON. About as much as Punch feels. That Garrick himself gave in to this foppery of feelings I can easily believe; but he knew at the same time that he lied. He might think it right, as far as I know, to have what fools imagined he ought to have. But it is amazing that any one should be so ignorant as to think that an actor will risk his reputation by depending on the feelings that shall be excited in the presence of two hundred people, on the repetition of certain words which he has repeated two hundred times before in what actors call their study. No, Sir. Garrick left nothing to chance. Every gesture, every expression of countenance and variation of voice, was settled in his closet before he set his foot upon the stage.

APPENDIX I

REYNOLDS ON SHAKESPEARE

As a critic of Shakespeare Sir Joshua made his *début* in 1765, when five of his notes were printed in the last volume of Johnson's edition of Shakespeare. Two other notes, one on *Macbeth*, one on *Lear*, were included in Malone's supplement (1780) to the edition of 1778. As the documents which follow prove, Reynolds was also engaged in writing an essay on Shakespeare, an essay which was never published because it was never completed. One wonders whether it was started in the expectation that Malone would print it. Such an hypothesis might explain the cryptic comment made by Boswell in a letter which he wrote to Malone in December, 1790: "Sir Joshua is pleased [with Malone's *Shakespeare*, which had just been published], though he would gladly have seen more *disquisition*—you understand me!"

That Sir Joshua was an original critic can hardly be said. Whether he is discussing theories of painting or theories of literature his opinions reflect the best thoughts of the best neo-classic writers. This is not to say that he did not think for himself. But in criticism as in other respects he was no innovator. What he says of Shakespeare in the following pages differs little from what was being written in his boyhood by the better critics, or in his manhood by Samuel Johnson. The chief point Reynolds makes, a defence of tragicomedy, had in fact already been made by Johnson himself. And yet the ideas which Sir Joshua has absorbed from others and has mulled over re-emerge in a very real sense as his own.

In a letter to Malone written in 1797 Burke discusses Sir Joshua's "disposition to abstractions, generalisations and classifications." This disposition is revealed in many of his notes which have survived. Among the Boswell Papers, for example, is the following:

> Whatever art or science, whatever pursuit engages the attention, a desire naturally arises to an inquisitive mind not only of forming a distinct idea of what the perfection of that art or science consists, but likewise of knowing by what proof or criterion this idea of excellence is ascertained. The mind naturally endeavours to extricate itself from the mazes of uncertainty, to find something on which it may securely repose and lean on. The truth of science is examined and known by reason. But arts have little to do with reason. They address themselves to another faculty; their whole commerce is with the imagination. Hence arises that appearance of uncertainty of truth in art, from the variety of opinions in matters of taste, and the difficulty of confutation of falsehood.

Here we see his inquisitive mind working on the fundamentals of the arts in general. Though his published writings pertain chiefly to painting, he was prone to draw analogies from the other arts, particularly from literature, and it is therefore not surprising that he should be attracted to the criticism of Shakespeare. In a preliminary note headed *Shakespeare* we find him turning to other arts for illustrative material.

> To take care particularly to guard yourself against the errors which we have a natural propensity to fall into. Art has a wonderful propensity to insipidity. A regular system is not so pleasant as a desultory observation, a regular built city or house as a chance city or improved [?improvised] house. *Cato*[1] is

[1] Addison's *Cato* had received extravagant praise. Reynolds here echoes what Johnson wrote in his *Preface to Shakespeare*: "*Cato* affords a splendid exhibition of artificial and fictitious manners and delivers just and noble sentiments in diction easy, elevated, and harmonious, but its hopes and fears communicate no vibration to the heart; the composition refers us only to the writer; we pronounce the name of Cato, but we think on Addison."

cold; Shakespeare the contrary. Art in its most perfect state is when it possesses those accidents which do not belong to the code of laws for that art. Poussin is too artificial in his draperies, perhaps in the whole. Carlo Maratti the same. Raphael's right taste makes him introduce accidental folds, &c.

A number of such notes have survived, some of which without doubt would have been expanded and incorporated into his essay on Shakespeare if that essay had been completed. As it is, we have unformed or partly developed ideas not yet articulated. It is an essay in embryo. But enough has survived to give us a good idea of his general argument, and it is worth reading as a sample of what the cultured gentleman of the eighteenth century had to say on the subject.

I do not pretend that the order in which the various fragments are here arranged is the order in which Sir Joshua would have arranged them. The opening paragraph can be said with some confidence to be Sir Joshua's opening, and the conclusion is so labelled. Between these two parts I have placed the others in what approximates a logical order, my chief aim being to include all the fragments.

The manuscript was dispersed, probably soon after Sir Joshua's death. A few pages are now to be found in the Royal Academy, others are in my possession, but the greatest number passed into Boswell's hands and are now with the Boswell Papers at Yale. To give the newly discovered manuscripts meaning I have here fitted them in with those that have already been published. Divorced from each other for a century and a half, the comments on Shakespeare are once more reunited.

APPENDIX I

Whoever opposes popular opinions is walking on "the unsteady footing of a spear".[1] The multitude of minds which have co-operated to the establishment of such public opinion, and who may be supposed to have examined the question at every view, must carry an authority which no individual can expect will be paid to himself.

Dr. Johnson has with great modesty and, he says himself, with a trembling hand when he considers what authorities are against him, vindicated Shakespeare in his neglect of the unities of time and place. How much greater apprehensions ought a man of less critical authority to entertain, when he endeavours to vindicate the same author in a breach of the established rules of criticism in a matter of perhaps still greater consequence, that of mixing tragedy and comedy. Such a new undertaking must have the appearance to a foreigner, especially to a Frenchman, as if the English had no other ideas of excellence than what Shakespeare afforded them and that they were resolved to vindicate his whole conduct, right or wrong, and not content to excuse his defects but even convert his faults into beauties. Convinced and aware of this hypercriticism which is to attend us, we will still venture to look about and see what can be said in the defence of this practice.

If the natural unsophisticated feelings of mankind are not on my side I have no resort. I appeal only to those. I am well

[1] I'll read thee matter deep and dangerous,
As full of peril and advent'rous spirit,
As to o'erwalk a current, roaring loud,
On the unsteadfast footing of a spear.

I Henry IV, I. iii.

Shakespearean quotations in these notes are from Johnson's edition of 1765.

aware all critics are of another party, and if I were to add they are fee'd by the other side, I should speak what I believe—that is, they think the credit of their critical skill depends on their supporting that opinion, for it must be acknowledged that the critics from [ ][1] down to Dryden have universally condemned this mixture. And as to the feelings of mankind, they will say: "We have every reason to suppose we have those on our side, for it is on this ground that those rules were instituted by the critics, who are the representatives, or more properly speaking, the judges, whose business it is to sum up the evidence of the senses or feelings of mankind." This undoubtedly has a most formidable appearance. I still think that if every soldier would act as if the whole victory depended upon himself—that is, judge from his own feelings—this formidable phalanx will not appear so terrible.

It may be justly said in opposition to our opinion that if this universally received opinion is not founded on nature, how came it to be first received and continue its existence in all codes of criticism? In answer to this it may be observed that works precede criticism and that few writers are capable of writing both comedy and tragedy. Being thus from accident or incapacity separate, the succeeding critics think they ought to be separate, and much good sense and reason may be brought forward to show the propriety of this separation, in which argument reason alone, not the passions, are consulted. Every man acquiesces to those reasons, and the rule is established. But if there should arise a genius of such magnitude

[1] Blank in MS.

and comprehension equal at least to any of those great men who first suggested to the critics this idea of separating comedy and tragedy, who is equally capable of carrying both to their highest excellence, who could have no prejudice in favour of rules which he never knew, but whose sagacity and general knowledge of human nature served in their stead, and who from the circumstance of his life had been always to the theatre and from his great sagacity knew the art of captivating the audience, drew his rules therefore from nature herself and not at second hand, it may be a question worthy the consideration of critics whether this civilised age does not demand a new code of laws and a thorough examination of those principles on which the contrary practice is founded.

Whether that mixture of grave and gay, the grandeur of general ideas with the familiar pathetic, the artful with the artless—that is, finished passages with the most simple and natural expressions and such as every man would use on the same occasion—is it not worth the pains for philosophers and playwrights to examine the cause why we are so delighted with Shakespeare's plays? From universal approbation is it not time to make a new code, to be out of our apprenticeship, acknowledging with all gratitude the assistance we have received from our masters the ancients, whose works have enabled us at this minute to stand upon our own legs, have taught us to walk?

To know what human nature is, to know the history of man, we wish to consider the manners of savages, men who have had no communication with others, in order to distinguish between imitation and what is inherent in our natures. All our works are conducted on a principle of imitation, a very good principle to begin with, but a very bad one to finish with. A man appears who instead of examining what others had done suggests from his own mind a mode that appears congenial to human nature, with what success we need say nothing.

Shakespeare is like a picture full of anachronisms—geographical blunders, forgetfulness of his plot, and even sometimes of character—but he produces a high-valued picture because his mind is intent upon the general effect.

We dislike artificial regularity. A writer, though he is perfectly acquainted with all the rules of correct writing, will run the risk of being even ungrammatical in order to preserve the idiom of the language and to give an air of facility.

The effect of a picture depends upon the background. The grace and effect of writing depends upon the place, the occasion. Words and expressions are fit for one person, not another. Nothing is right *per se*.

What is particularly to be insisted on in regard to Shakespeare is that genius which pervades his works—that is, possessing a mind that conceived vigorously and impressed that conception on his readers. As a man who is pursuing or engaged in some object with an interest as if his life depended on it will, by a thousand undesirable actions and tones of voice, possess the hearers with a sympathetic feeling, so are the characters of Shakespeare. We are acquainted with them and know what they would do upon every occasion as well as we do our acquaintance.[1]

[1] One of Sir Joshua's notes in the Boswell Papers reads: "How many general characters, which will always exist in the mind, are to be found in Shakespeare!"

Shakespeare seems to expect this from his readers, for like Pindar he does not stoop to a cold explanation of his intention in the character, though perhaps a single line would be enough, but concluding that you are possessed with the character as much as he was himself.

From this source arise many of the difficulties of Shakespeare, a stumbling block to the learner and a smooth path to ignorance. Thus Polonius; thus the passage in *Othello*:

Nature could not invest, &c.[1]

Shakespeare has given what may be called sketches of characters which escape in the representation or on superficial reading. He wished to introduce so great a variety, there is not time to finish any of them, or at least not all of them. As he sometimes appears to have wrote for the vulgar, at other times he seems to have formed a higher opinion of the judgment and sagacity of his audience than a man writing for a mixed multitude ought perhaps to entertain.

[1] "Nature would not invest herself in such shadowing passion without some instruction. It is not words that shake me thus—pish—noses, ears, and lips—is't possible!—confess!—handkerchief!—oh devil "(*Othello*, IV. i). The passage called forth a long conjectural note by Warburton. To this Reynolds replied in the following note, included in the appendix to Johnson's edition: "However ingenious Dr. Warburton's note may be, it is certainly too forced and far-fetched. Othello alludes only to Cassio's dream, which had been invented and told him by Iago, when many confused and very interesting ideas pour in upon the mind all at once, and with such rapidity, that it has not time to shape or digest them. If the mind does not relieve itself by tears, which we know it often does, whether for joy or grief, it produces stupefaction and fainting. Othello, in broken sentences and single words, all of which have a reference to the cause of his jealousy, shows that all the proofs are present at once to his mind, which so overpowers it, that he falls in a trance, the natural consequence."

Of this I think many instances might be produced of a refined conception of character which may have a great chance of being overlooked.

Of this kind, I think, is Jaques, for though one of the characters calls him the melancholy Jaques, that is not his character, nor so intended by Shakespeare. And here, by the by, is an instance of that respect he paid to his audience in supposing they would form their own opinion and not rest on the opinion which another character in the play gives of him, but that they would form their opinion from the general representation of the character. He is not a melancholy man but appears to have taken an improper disgust to society from the coxcombs and pretenders that from their forwardness are caressed and take the lead in society. "I think," says he, "of as many things as they do, but I thank God I make no boast of them"—that is, "I do not seek knowledge in order to parade it in company, but to be really wiser."[1]

When Jaques heard the fool moralise, "in good set phrases,[2] and yet," says he, "a motley fool," he exults in the idea. It was a treat to him, as it fed that disgust which he had taken to the paraders in conversation. He insists much on that, "in good set phrases, and yet a motley fool."

There is the same nicety in the character of Pandarus and Cressida among other excellencies that appear to be overlooked, or at least not likely to be observed in vulgar criticism.

[1] "I think of as many matters as he, but I give heaven thanks, and make no boast of them" (*As You Like It*, II. v).

[2] Sir Joshua changes the metre. Jaques says:

"In good set terms—and yet a motley fool" (*As You Like It*, II. vii).

APPENDIX I

The character of Cressida is of the highest order of courtesan—a great deal of what is called snipsnap wit and repartee, seeing with great quickness the ridicule of character and always endeavouring to make something out of nothing. In this view consider the scene between her and Pandarus [in Act I] when the Grecian heroes pass in review on the stage.

To observe of Shakespeare that he observed everything that passed before him and considered it with a poetical mind, and that he took his ideas from nature herself, would be superfluous praise. I would only observe that by considering nature as a poet, he involuntarily considered it as a painter. His descriptions are pictures: Dover Cliff; "her head sometimes on one side, sometimes on t'other";[1] "clear sky of fame."[2] He appears to have looked at the human face like a painter who wishes to imprint on his memory the movements of the features when any particular character was expressed: "peeping through their little eyes";[3] "swell their cheeks to idle merri-

[1] The references are to the famous description in *King Lear* (IV. vi) and the following:

> To me comes a creature,
> Sometimes her head on one side, some another,
> I never saw a vessel of like sorrow
> So filled, and so becoming; in pure white robes
> Like very sanctity, she did approach
> My cabin where I lay.
>
> *Winter's Tale*, III. iii.

[2] "If you do not all show like gilt twopences to me, and I, in the clear sky of fame, o'ershine you as much as the full moon doth the cinders of the element . . . believe not the word of a noble" (*II Henry IV*, IV. vi).

[3] Some that will evermore peep through their eyes,
And laugh like parrots, at a bag-piper. *Merchant of Venice*, I. i.

"This", notes Warburton, "gives us a very picturesque image of the countenance in laughing, when the eyes appear half shut."

ment."[1] The frown of the forehead, and the expression of the eyes in consequence, had been observed before, but "a napkin ill laid up—"[2]

The business of art is rationally to amuse us and not send us to school. If it is, we should go unwilling to school.[3] We must be recreated with variety. The breezy comedy of Shakespeare is founded on nature.

I hold that Shakespeare's being such a favourite proceeds in a great measure from what the critics considered as faults. I am an advocate for criticism as founded on nature.

When a great genius has continued for ages to please, and to please by means contrary to the established art of pleasing, it is then high time to overhaul the rules of art, that they pass a new examination, that they be made more agreeable to the nature of man.

The practice of Shakespeare demands this respect—a shrewd mind, forming the rules of his art not from authority but from the impressions that he observed were made on the audience. Critics come afterwards and examine the conduct of his drama by the rules already received and established, and finding but little conformity to those rules, do not hesitate a moment to pronounce Shakespeare guilty, upon a supposition

[1] Making that idiot laughter keep men's eyes
And strain their cheeks to idle merriment. *King John*, III. v.

[2] "O, you shall see him laugh, till his face be like a wet cloak ill laid up" (*II Henry IV*, V. i).

[3] And then, the whining school-boy with his satchel,
And shining morning-face, creeping like snail
Unwillingly to school.
As You Like It, II. ix.

that he has enough (which is true too) to support the character of the greatest genius. Acknowledging this defect, I must remark here that I do not wish to vindicate Shakespeare in all points, but only the mixture of serious with comic characters.

Theoretical systems appear to have a great propensity to separate in theory what is inseparable in nature. They go on a supposition that by their precepts and orders they can give a different disposition and quality to the mind than nature had thought proper to give, that a man ought totally to keep separate his intellectual from his sensual desires. All this is fine theory, but—

Man being what he is, an inconsistent being, a professed lover of art and nature, of order, of regularity, and of variety, and who therefore cannot long continue his attention without some recreation; hence it is that the poet relieves the mind of the reader, professedly by episodes, and in a more private manner by similes and illustrations, with which he proceeds so far that it would be open to ridicule but for this reason of variety. Thus Milton and Homer.

The principles of poetry are certainly formed upon such conduct as by experience is found to please, but I suspect that the rigid forms to be observed in tragedy, of admitting nothing that shall divert and recreate, is formed upon what we ought to like if we were endued with perfect wisdom and taste. But that is not the case. We are governed by our passions as well as our reason.

Man is both a consistent and an inconsistent being, a lover of art when it imitates nature and of nature when it imitates art, of uniformity and of variety, a creature of habit that loves novelty. The principles of art must conform to this capricious being, and it may be worth considering how much it does conform.

Critics seem to consider man as too uniformly wise, and in their rules make no account for the playful part of the mind. Their rules are formed for another race of beings than what man really is. They do not form their rules always from experience of what does please, but what they in their great wisdom think ought to please—as if they should say man ought to like what is regular only, his passion for variety is vicious.

The mind appears to me of that nature and construction that it requires being employed on two things in order that it may do one thing well. Perhaps this disposition proceeds from the mind having always been accustomed to do many things at once, as in reading and writing, in which, from long habit, the operation of the mind comes to be no operation, or at least not perceptible. This double operation, what it has been so long accustomed to, begins at last to be a thing necessary, and required even, in affairs where a man would wish the whole powers of his mind to concentrate. Hence I would infer that that simplicity which is so much boasted in the ancient drama, or in whatever works of imagination, is even not natural to the mind of man. If I was to judge from my own experience, the mind always desires to double, to entertain two objects at a time.

This may fairly extend itself to tragicomedy.

There is nothing of the character and disposition of the mind that we know with more certainty than that it has a pleasure and gratification in a certain activity and exertion of its faculties. But this is a gratification only when the exertion is light and moderate, in the same manner as the body requires motion after a long continuance in rest.

The theatre acts as a flapper and rouses in us for the time a fictitious feeling of interest and pleasing anxiety. The feelings excited at the theatre, though they may be of the same genus with distress in life, their different magnitude make them not of the same species, no more than a fillip with the finger and thumb is of the same kind as a blow with a Herculean club. The effect of one is over as soon as given; the other affects you hours, days, perhaps through your whole life. There is this difference between a real misfortune and a fictitious one.

The objection, then, to the succession of comic after tragic scenes vanishes if it goes upon a supposition that the feelings are as heavy and as durable as in life.

After a long serious attention the mind wants relief by variety; variety we are sure is a very predominant disposition of the mind. The contrast required to sorrow is mirth. From those opposites, artificial and opposed to each other, proceeds, as in music from discords, that harmony which is the delight of the soul.

The argument against this variety, this sprinkling, this relief of the attention from mournful scenes, is that it destroys the interest in the great object of the scene. This argument goes upon a supposition that our interest is more real, makes a greater impression on our mind, and is even a deception to it, more than it in reality is.

To refer to our habits, to what we are used to at a table: after you have heard a long melancholy story of a murder attended with pathetic circumstances, but such as do not any more refer to yourself than a theatrical representation, after the conversation has for some time taken this turn, would a lively, entertaining, or even merry story come amiss or be ill received by the company? But the contrary is not equally true, that a merry company, crossed by a melancholy story, will be well received. Hence it is that a dash of comedy succeeds in a tragedy, as was Shakespeare's practice, but neither he nor anyone else has endeavoured to introduce tragic circumstances in a comedy. The truth is, a man does not willingly receive any obstruction to his mirth, but is very glad to have his melancholy mood removed as fast as it can. A little is enough, just sufficient to serve as a shade of variety. So the lightness of mirth.

Conclusion

All the apologies which Dr. Johnson has thought it necessary to make for our poet's neglect of the unities of time and place are equally necessary for the admission of that monster (as it is often called)[1] of tragicomedy into civilised society. It has undoubtedly the appearance of making a universal sacrifice of the wisdom of ages, the practice of poets, to the shrine of an individual poet.

[1] One of Sir Joshua's notes in the Boswell Papers reads: "As if tragicomedy was a monster that ought not to be suffered to exist in a civilized country!" Sir Joshua's friend William Mason wrote in his *Life of Gray* (1775): "Mr. Gray always thought highly of [Southerne's] pathetic powers, at the same time that he blamed his ill taste for mixing them so injudiciously with farce, in order to produce that monstrous species of composition called tragicomedy."

APPENDIX I

If the rules of epic poetry are formed from the practice of Homer, and those of tragedy from Sophocles and Euripides, and of comedy from Menander and Terence, and if a new and great genius has arisen equal to any of them and superior for universality of powers, with success superior to what was ever before seen, and upon a plan in the general construction totally different, it is time for a new code of laws, or at least for the old to be fairly and candidly revised.

APPENDIX II

THE IRONICAL DISCOURSE

In the closing years of Sir Joshua's life the chief topic of conversation everywhere was the French Revolution. In politics Reynolds was a Whig. He had been in sympathy with the colonists during the American Revolution. But by temperament he was an arch-conservative, a pupil of Dr. Johnson's, a product of the neo-classic school. Like his close friend Burke, he naturally shifted to the Tory side and, in the words of Malone, "frequently avowed his contempt of those 'Adam-wits' who set at nought the accumulated wisdom of ages, and on all occasions are desirous of beginning the world anew." If Farington's opinion is true in general, that Sir Joshua lacked strong feelings, it is certainly false with reference to the upheaval across the Channel.

Burke published his *Reflections on the French Revolution* on the first of November, 1790. Before it was in print he had read it to Reynolds, who was, says Malone, "lavish in his encomiums upon it." It was at this time that Sir Joshua was writing his fifteenth and last discourse, which he delivered to the students at the Royal Academy on the tenth of December. In it he reviewed what he had said in previous lectures and strengthened the position which he had consistently maintained, that what the world calls inspiration is the result of hard work. "It is an ancient saying, that labour is the price which the gods have set upon every thing valuable." Between the lines one can read Sir Joshua's hostility to the "new" school of artists, to men like William Blake, who were of course radical in politics as well as in theories of art.[1] "I am aware," writes Reynolds, "how much

[1] " 'Well, Mr. Blake,' blandly remarked the President, who, doubtless, had heard strange accounts of his interlocutor's sayings and doings, 'I hear you despise our art of oil-painting.' 'No, Sir Joshua, I don't despise it; but I like fresco better.' "

by this advice I have laid myself open to the sarcasms of those critics who imagine our art to be a matter of inspiration."

Throughout 1791 the tension mounted between radical and conservative. Sir Joshua, whose near-blindness prevented him from painting, felt himself more and more impelled to express in writing his ideas on the sorry state in which the world found itself. The two men with whom he was most closely associated at this time were Burke and Malone. Burke, as is well known, was devoting all his energies to the cause. Malone's attitude is best brought out by a note which he wrote several years later to what Reynolds had said of the Luxemburg Gallery: "This was written before France had been disgraced, and plundered, and desolated, by the unparalleled atrocities of those sanguinary and ferocious savages who for seven years past have deluged that country with blood; while they have waged war against every principle that binds man to man: against all the arts and all the elegancies of life; against beauty, virtue, law, social order, true liberty, religion, and even humanity itself." Malone added that the collection of the Duke of Orleans had been "fortunately saved from their merciless fangs by the necessities and precaution of the owner, the detestable author and fomenter of their iniquities; who, happily for the world, though most cruelly, basely, and unjustly, so far as regards the perpetrators of the act, was some time since worried and mangled by those hell-hounds which he let loose against mankind."

Characteristically Sir Joshua preferred a less direct attack. It occurred to him that his most effective vehicle would be a discourse, written as for the students of the Royal Academy, in which he should praise the new and ridicule the conservative position. His friends encouraged him, and in the summer of 1791 he drafted his lecture. The date of composition is inferred from the fact that the discourse is written on the backs of pages of the fair copy of the fifteenth discourse and of a draft of the letter dated 15 June that Sir Joshua published in *The Gentleman's Magazine* for July, 1791. The discourse, then, was probably written after the middle of June and before October, when his health prevented him from concentrating on any task.

THE IRONICAL DISCOURSE

Students of neo-classic theories of art will find the ironical discourse the most delightful of the manuscripts here printed. Its existence had not even been suspected. Malone must have discussed it with Reynolds, since he was helping Sir Joshua prepare a collected edition of his writings. And, from what Reynolds says in his introduction, Malone must have known that Sir Joshua wished it to be printed as a sixteenth discourse. But his decision to exclude it from his edition of Sir Joshua's writings was justifiable, since it is a rough draft which was presumably never finished. Readers of today should bear this in mind. The irony is heavy-handed. It lacks the polish of Sir Joshua's published work.

The discourse is none the less interesting. It sharply sums up what Sir Joshua had written on the arts in his letters to the *Idler* thirty-two years earlier and what he had stressed in all of his discourses. His Johnsonian definition of genius in the second discourse ("assiduity unabated by difficulty, and a disposition eagerly directed to the object of its pursuit"), his reverence for the great men who had preceded him, his insistence that "the minute peculiarities of dress" are distracting, that "the general idea constitutes real excellence"—these basic ideas are here given a reverse twist which makes them more emphatic. Amusingly enough Sir Joshua seems to have felt in two instances that his irony might be misunderstood. His real opinions of the value of rules and of Pliny's criticism appear in footnotes which he has added to the text.

The ironical discourse reveals the basic differences between the old order and the new at the close of the eighteenth century. At times it reminds one of the annotations which, a few years later, William Blake was to make in his copy of Sir Joshua's writings. But if Reynolds had an individual in mind, it was not Blake, but James Barry, who as Professor of Painting in the Academy had pointedly attacked the President. Sir Joshua told Northcote that "as many of Barry's discoveries were new to himself, so he thought they were new to every body else." At the outset of the ironical discourse Reynolds refers to a bright genius who sneered at the pains a writer had taken in composing a discourse. It recalls Northcote's anecdote of Barry's rudeness to Reynolds. When Sir Joshua rightly scolded

Barry for his procrastination in delivering his lectures, the young painter, "with his fist clenched in a menacing posture," replied: "If I had no more to do in the composition of my lectures than to produce such poor flimsy stuff as your discourses, I should soon have done my work."

SIR JOSHUA'S PREFACE

THE following ironical discourse owes its origin to a conversation on Burke's *Reflections on the Revolution of France*, of which book Sir Joshua Reynolds expressed the most enthusiastic admiration, both in regard to the doctrine which it contained, and the eloquence in which that doctrine was conveyed.

The conversation turned on the power which is lodged in majorities. It was said that the French nation having almost unanimously adopted the revolution had in its favour this greatest criterion of truth. This inference was disputed. Sir Joshua was of opinion that if matters of taste are determined as he thinks they ought to be, by weight rather than by tale, much more political questions, which involved so much science, ought to be determined by the few learned in that art, and not by the ignorant majority.

That the majority were ignorant was denied, and much was said of the "present enlightened age," and on the general diffusion of knowledge amongst all ranks of people. They were therefore capable of judging for themselves. They had tasted of the tree of knowledge: they now knew good from evil, and would not take it as they had done. That [they had tasted] of the tree of knowledge was granted, but they had only tasted and, it appears, as much to their own loss as 'twas to our first parents. Our poet says, "Drink deep, or taste not."[1]

This tree of knowledge, on which they pretend to say that mankind now have battened, does not grow upon a new made, slender soil, but is fastened by strong roots to ancient rocks, and is the slow growth of ages. There are but few of strength sufficient to climb the summit of this rock, from whence indeed they may look down to us and clouds below.

It was acknowledged that more people could read and write and cast accounts than in any former age, and that more people read newspapers, magazines, &c. But it was not to be inferred from thence that this smattering of knowledge capacitated them to set up for legislators, or to measure, separate, and balance exactly rational liberty against sound and necessary restraint; or, in regard to taste and skill in arts, that we were a jot the nearer to see a Michael Angelo, Raphael, Titian, or Correggio, because there were at present a greater number of middling artists than at any other period;[2] or, because we have more dabblers in poetry, that there is a greater probability of our seeing arise amongst us [a] Homer or a Milton.

It is now as it ever has been. Few people reach the summit from which they look down on the rest of mankind. However it may be in arithmetic, in such studies ever so many additions of units will not possess the efficacy of the compact number of

[1] A little learning is a dang'rous thing;
Drink deep, or taste not the Pierian spring.
Pope's *Essay on Criticism*.

[2] Compare the first discourse: "There are, at this time, a greater number of excellent artists than were ever known before at one period in this nation".

twenty[1]. A hundred thousand near-sighted men, that see only what is just before them, make no equivalent to one man whose view extends to the whole horizon round him, though we may safely acknowledge at the same time that like the real near-sighted men, they see and comprehend as distinctly what is within the focus of their sight as accurately (I will allow sometimes more accurately) than the others. Though a man may see his way in the management of his own affairs, within his own little circle, with the greatest acuteness and sagacity, such habits give him no pretensions to set up for a politician. So far is this diffusion of superficial knowledge from being an argument of our superiority in the deeper recesses of science, that on the contrary we hear it continually given as a reason why there are not at present such learned men as in former ages, from this very circumstance—that every man, having a mouthful (just enough to save himself from an intellectual famine), does not take the pains necessary to get a bellyful.[2] If this be true, the diffusion of knowledge is against them, instead of an argument in their favour. It was asked likewise whether, from a little smattering in physic, a

[1] Compare the fourth discourse: "However contradictory it may be in geometry, it is true in taste, that many little things will not make a great one".

[2] The metaphor is Johnson's. A cancelled passage reads: "To go on with Johnson's metaphor, we may say: in this general diffusion of intellectual provisions, have we any of so capacious a stomach, such powers of digestion, as some of the giants of former ages, such as Bacon, Newton, Selden, or Locke?" In 1776 was published a small volume entitled *Johnsoniana; or, a Collection of Bon Mots, &c.* On the third page Johnson is quoted as saying of the Scotch: "I grant you they have all a *mouthful* of learning, but not one of them a *bellyful.*" A year earlier Johnson had confirmed to Boswell the authenticity of the remark and a year later Mrs. Thrale notes that the story "is so well known it is not worth recording."

man would act wisely in discarding his physicians and prescribe to himself, whether by such quacking, sound constitutions have not been often destroyed.

Sir Joshua added, that to be a politician was, he apprehended, as much a trade or profession as his own: that the science of politics, as well as a true taste in works of art, was acquired by labour and study, and by other means; and that in both cases, we are sure that half-educated minds are in a worse state than total ignorance: the worst will appear the best, as being within their narrow comprehension.[1] He instanced a certain painter now in England, an artist of great merit, though he paints in a different and a much inferior style to Vandyck; yet if the merit of each of them was to be determined by the majority, there would be 99 in 100 in favour of this artist.

He proceeded to observe [that] he would undertake to write a discourse on those obvious and vulgar principles, which should come home to the bosoms[2] of the ignorant (which are always the majority) and which should be thought to contain more sound doctrine than those which he had delivered in the Academy; and such doctrine, proceeding *ex cathedra*, would probably so poison the minds of the students as might eventually keep back the harvest of arts which we expect from the nation, perhaps for fifty years. A few days after was produced the following discourse, which, though a playful trifle, he is persuaded by his friends to let it bring up the rear of his last volume, as they

[1] Compare the fifth discourse: "It is certain that the lowest style will be the most popular, as it falls within the compass of ignorance itself".

[2] Compare the dedication to Bacon's *Essays*: "my Essays . . . come home to men's business and bosoms."

think it may contribute towards banishing from the world the popular and vulgar notions about genius and inspiration, as well as those opinions which have been entertained both by the great vulgar and the small, of what ought to be the object of art.[1]

[1] Parallel passages make dull reading. Nevertheless the ironical discourse loses much of its meaning if the reader is unaware of what Reynolds had said in his published discourses. To supply this meaning, passages which Reynolds obviously had in mind are, from this point on, printed on the page facing the text. They may, however, be disregarded by any reader who wishes to do so, and perhaps had best be disregarded in the first reading of the discourse. All references are to volume and page of the second edition of Sir Joshua's *Works*, edited by Malone and published in 1798.

THE DISCOURSE

Gentlemen:

It is with great regret that I see so many students labouring day after day in the Academy, as if they imagined that a liberal art, as ours is, was to be acquired like a mechanical trade,[a] by dint of labour, or I may add the absurdity of supposing that it could be acquired by any means whatever.[b] We know that if you are born with a genius, labour is unnecessary; if you have it not, labour is in vain; genius is all in all.[c] It was wittily said by a bright genius, who observed another to labour in the composition of a discourse which he was to deliver in public, that such a painstaker was fitter to make a pulpit than to preach in it.

Genius, as it disdains all assistance, so it defies all obstacles. The student here may inform himself whether he has been favoured by heaven with this truly divine gift.[d] If he finds it necessary to copy, to study the works of other painters, or any way to seek for help out of himself, he may be sure that he has received nothing of that inspiration. My advice is that he immediately quit the Academy, and apply to something to which his genius is adapted. Let the student consider with himself whether he is impelled forward by irresistible instinct. He himself is little more than a machine,[e] unconscious of the power

[a] Compare the fourth discourse: "The value and rank of every art is in proportion to the mental labour employed in it, or the mental pleasure produced by it. As this principle is observed or neglected, our profession becomes either a liberal art, or a mechanical trade" (i. 79).

[b] Compare the sixth discourse: "Those who have undertaken to write on our art, and have represented it as a kind of *inspiration*, as a *gift* bestowed upon peculiar favourites at their birth, seem to insure a much more favourable disposition from their readers, and have a much more captivating and liberal air, than he who attempts to examine, coldly, whether there are any means by which this art may be acquired" (i. 147).

[c] Compare the sixth discourse: "Genius is supposed to be a power of producing excellencies, which are out of the reach of the rules of art; a power which no precepts can teach, and which no industry can acquire" (i. 152).

[d] Compare the third discourse: "As if they could not sufficiently express their admiration of his genius by what they knew, they have recourse to poetical enthusiasm; they call it inspiration, a gift from heaven" (i. 53).

[e] Compare the seventh discourse: "To understand literally these metaphors or ideas expressed in poetical language seems to be equally absurd as to conclude that because painters sometimes represent poets writing from the dictates of a little winged boy or genius, that this same genius did really inform him in a whisper what he was to write; and that he is himself but a mere machine, unconscious of the operations of his own mind" (i. 195).

which impels him forward to the instant performance of what others learn by the slow method of rules and precepts. Who does not feel the highest disdain for all the *imitatores servum pecus*[1] as well as the most sovereign contempt for all rules, or rather receipts, which dullness have prescribed for the acquisition of this great and liberal art?[a]

What is the use of rules, but to cramp and fetter genius?[b] The rules which dull men have introduced into liberal arts smother that flame which would otherwise blaze out in originality of invention.[c] Shakespeare, as the great Ralph says, writ without rules. (Quote the note of the *Dunciad*. He made the following wise answer.)[2] The idea of making a work of genius by rule has been sufficiently laughed at. (Swift in his receipt[3] to make an epic poem.)[4]

One is at a loss, says the great Bacon, to determine which was the greater trifler[5] [Apelles or Albert Dürer, "whereof the

[1] MS: *imitatores servi pecus*. The phrase (imitators, slavish herd) is from Horace's *Epistles*, I. xix. Peter Pindar in his *Lyric Ode to the Royal Academy* (1782) referred to the many imitators of Sir Joshua as

> Imps, who just boast the merit of *Translators*—
> Horace's *servum pecus*—*Imitators*.

[2] The words in round brackets refer to the following note by Pope (*Dunciad*, III. 165): "James Ralph . . . was wholly illiterate and knew no language, not even *French*. Being advised to read the rules of dramatic poetry before he began a play, he smiled and replied, 'Shakespeare writ without rules.' "

[3] At this point in the MS. Reynolds added the following note: "It is without doubt open to ridicule, to imagine that by receipt *alone* any kind of excellence be produced, but a bad use would be made of this jest, if we were to imagine it extended to invalidate the efficacy of precepts and the wholesome restraints of rules of art. Rules act negatively. It does not produce good as much as it prevents evil, like the ten commandments."

[4] *See* chapter xv of the *Art of Sinking in Poetry*.

[5] The MS. does not include the passage from Bacon's essay *Of Beauty*, which Reynolds quoted in the third discourse.

[a] Compare the sixth discourse: "To derive all from native power, to owe nothing to another, is the praise which men who do not much think on what they are saying bestow sometimes upon others, and sometimes on themselves: and their imaginary dignity is naturally heightened by a supercilious censure of the low, the barren, the grovelling, the servile imitator. It would be no wonder if a student, frightened by these terrific and disgraceful epithets, with which the poor imitators are so often loaded, should let fall his pencil in mere despair (conscious as he must be, how much he has been indebted to the labours of others, how little, how very little of his art was born with him); and consider it as hopeless to set about acquiring by the imitation of any human master what he is taught to suppose is matter of inspiration from heaven" (i. 149).

[b] Compare the first discourse: ". . . that false and vulgar opinion, that rules are the fetters of genius; they are fetters only to men of no genius; as that armour which upon the strong is an ornament and a defence, upon the weak and mis-shapen becomes a load, and cripples the body which it was made to protect" (i. 12).

[c] Compare the sixth discourse: "Genius has been compared to a spark of fire which is smothered by a heap of fuel, and prevented from blazing into a flame" (i. 160).

one would make a personage by geometrical proportions; the other, by taking the best parts out of divers faces to make one excellent."][a] It is but too true that this weak observation is found in Bacon's *Essays*, as if he thought that there was no rule for beauty or proportion. Cardinal Bembo had a true idea of what the highest excellence consists, and in his epitaph on Raphael has flattered him as supposing he possessed it, but alas![b]

Having given my idea of genius, before I proceed to explain how it shows itself and what are its operations, it is necessary that you should be aware that our art is in a corrupted state, and has been gradually departing from simple first principles ever since the time of Michael Angelo, the first grand corrupter of the natural taste of man.[c] He first introduced and substituted this style founded on imagination, of which we may truly say there is not even the least gleam of common sense. The mere stating the question discovers its absurdity. What is cultivating the imagination, but to open a school to teach systematically madness and folly, and to renounce reason and even common sense?

It is not easy to account for the tame submission of mankind, either in first adopting this new style, or for its authority continuing to this present age. We can only put it to the account of a prejudice,[d] which perhaps originated from his being highly favoured by the popes and great men of his time and is handed down to our time. But shall we in these enlightened times tamely adopt and inherit their ignorant prejudices? No! Let us examine everything by the standard of

[a] Compare the third discourse: "Even the great Bacon treats with ridicule the idea of confining proportion to rules, or of producing beauty by selection. 'A man cannot tell (says he), whether Apelles or Albert Dürer were the more trifler: whereof the one . . .' " (i. 61).

[b] Compare the thirteenth discourse: "When such a man as Plato speaks of painting as only an imitative art, and that our pleasure proceeds from observing and acknowledging the truth of the imitation, I think he misleads us by a partial theory. It is in this poor, partial, and so far, false, view of the art, that Cardinal Bembo has chosen to distinguish even Raphael himself" (ii. 118). Bembo's epitaph is quoted at the end of Vasari's *Life of Raphael*.

[c] Compare the fifth discourse: "The reputation of this truly great man has been continually declining as the art itself has declined. For I must remark to you that it has long been much on the decline, and that our only hope of its revival will consist in your being thoroughly sensible of its depravation and decay. It is to Michael Angelo that we owe even the existence of Raphael. It is to him Raphael owes the grandeur of his style" (i. 127). And compare the fifteenth discourse: "That the art has been in a gradual state of decline from the age of Michael Angelo to the present must be acknowledged" (ii. 213).

[d] Compare the fifteenth discourse: "If the high esteem and veneration in which Michael Angelo has been held by all nations and in all ages should be put to the account of prejudice, it must still be granted that those prejudices could not have been entertained without a cause; the ground of our prejudice then becomes the source of our admiration" (ii. 216).

our own reason, renounce all prejudices for the reputed wisdom of others.[a] Let me ask any sensible artist who has seen the Cappella Sistina of Michael Angelo whether he found in the works of this great teacher of the nonsense of imagination that true nature which he had been taught to expect to find and which he knows he ought to find.[b]

It has been often remarked by many of our learned connoisseurs, that painters are the worst judges of pictures; and the reason why they are so, is from their imbibing prejudices. A man who never saw a picture is therefore the best judge. He has no rule but his taste and feeling. . . . [We should remember Apelles's critic] and Molière's old woman;[c] and above all, what that excellent philosopher and connoisseur Pliny[1] has recorded as the greatest effort of art of two of the greatest painters of antiquity, Zeuxis and Parrhasius, one painting a bunch of grapes that the birds pecked at and the other a curtain which deceived even the painter himself.[d] What a poor figure Michael Angelo would have made in this noble contention of superiority! We must not forget in more modern times Giotto's Circle.[2] These great masters knew

[1] At this point in the MS. Reynolds has added the following note: "Though the elder Pliny affords much information to the antiquarian in art, yet as a connoisseur he appears to be no great conjuror."

[2] The pope's messenger "repaired one morning to the workshop where Giotto was occupied with his labours. He declared the purpose of the pope, and the manner in which that pontiff desired to avail himself of his assistance, and finally requested to have a drawing, that he might send it to his holiness. Giotto, who was very courteous, took a sheet of paper and a pencil dipped in a red colour; then, resting his elbow on his side, to form a sort of compass, with one turn of the hand he drew a circle so perfect and exact that it was a marvel to behold. This done, he turned, smiling to the courtier, saying, 'Here is your

[a] Compare the seventh discourse: "In proportion as these prejudices are known to be generally diffused, or long received, the taste which conforms to them approaches nearer to certainty, and to a sort of resemblance to real science, even where opinions are found to be no better than prejudices. And since they deserve, on account of their duration and extent, to be considered as really true, they become capable of no small degree of stability" (i. 201).

[b] Compare the fifteenth discourse: "I would ask any man qualified to judge of such works, whether he can look with indifference at the personification of the Supreme Being in the centre of the Cappella Sistina . . . and whether the same sensations are not excited by those works, as what he may remember to have felt from the most sublime passages of Homer" (ii. 203).

[c] This phrase begins a new page. The page immediately preceding it has not been recovered. Compare the thirteenth discourse: "An ignorant, uneducated man may, like Apelles's critic, be a competent judge of the truth of the representation of a sandal; or to go somewhat higher, like Molière's old woman, may decide upon what is nature, in regard to comic humour; but a critic in the higher style of art ought to possess the same refined taste which directed the artist in his work" (ii. 120).

[d] Compare the fifth discourse: "Pliny, therefore, though we are under great obligations to him for the information he has given us in relation to the works of ancient artists, is very frequently wrong when he speaks of them, which he does very often in the style of many of our modern connoisseurs" (i. 119). The reference in the ironical discourse is to Pliny's *Natural History*, Bk. xxxv. chap. 36.

what was the real object of art, and went directly to the point. Nature herself was always at their elbow, and they wanted no other instruction.

Let the works in the Cappella Sistina—or to refer to what we have in our own nation, the vaunted cartoons[a]—let them be examined by the criterion of nature, and we shall be convinced how much the art has swerved from truth. Does any man, when he looks at those pictures, recognise his neighbour's face? Does anybody mistake the drapery, as it is called, for real stuff such as they are intended to represent? Is it silk, satin, or velvet?[b] What a falling off from the ancient simplicity of art! Let us imitate the great Mirabeau.[1] Set fire to all the pictures, prints, and drawings of Raphael and Michael Angelo; *non tali auxilio.*[2] Destroy every trace that remains of

---

drawing.' 'Am I to have nothing more than this?' inquired the latter, conceiving himself to be jested with. 'That is enough and to spare,' returned Giotto. 'Send it with the rest, and you will see if it will be recognised.' The messenger, unable to obtain any thing more, went away very ill-satisfied, and fearing that he had been fooled. Nevertheless, having despatched the other drawings to the pope, with the names of those who had done them, he sent that of Giotto also, relating the mode in which he had made his circle, without moving his arm and without compasses; from which the pope, and such of the courtiers as were well versed in the subject, perceived how far Giotto surpassed all the other painters of his time" (Vasari's *Life of Giotto*, translated by Mrs. Jonathan Foster).

[1] Mirabeau had died in April, 1791. In what follows, Sir Joshua probably had Dr. Johnson in mind. Among the manuscripts recovered at Malahide Castle were notes made by Reynolds when reading the *Lives of the Poets*. One of the passages which he transcribed from the *Life of Butler* reads: "The wisdom of the nation is very reasonably supposed to reside in the parliament. What can be concluded of the lower classes of the people when in one of the parliaments summoned by Cromwell it was seriously proposed that all the records in the Tower should be burnt, that all memory of things past should be effaced, and that the whole system of life should commence anew?"

[2] MS: *non talis auxilio*, here perhaps meaning "*They* are of no use to *us*!" The phrase is from Virgil (*Aeneid*, II. 521).

[a] Compare the thirteenth discourse: "The lower kind of comedy or farce, like the inferior style of painting, the more naturally it is represented, the better; but the higher appears to me to aim no more at imitation, so far as it belongs to any thing like deception, or to expect that the spectators should think that the events there represented are really passing before them, than Raphael in his cartoons, or Poussin in his Sacraments, expected it to be believed, even for a moment, that what they exhibited were real figures. For want of this distinction the world is filled with false criticism. Raphael is praised for naturalness and deception, which he certainly has not accomplished, and as certainly never intended" (ii. 130).

[b] Compare the fourth discourse: "It is the inferior style that marks the variety of stuffs. With [the historical painter] the clothing is neither woollen, nor linen, nor silk, satin, or velvet. It is drapery; it is nothing more" (i. 90).

ancient taste.[a] Let us pull the whole fabric down at once, root it up even to its foundation. Let us begin the art again upon this solid ground of nature and of reason.[b] The world will then see what naked art is, in its uneducated, unprejudiced, unadulterated state.

The daring to give this advice, the glory of stepping forth in this great work of reformation, and endeavouring to rescue the world from the worse than barbarous tyranny of prejudice, and restore the sovereignty of reason, will be sufficient honour for me and my poor endeavours.

I have only a few words to add respecting sculpture. As monuments are now erecting in St. Paul's,[1] I would recommend to the committee that the sculptor be obliged to dress his figures, whether one or many, in the very dress of the times—the dress which they themselves wore.[c] If this obliges the sculptor to acquire an accurate observation of the fashions as they fluctuate, this additional trouble will be fully compensated by [his] being saved another trouble, the disposition of the drapery, that being already done to his hands by the tailor.[d] And, by the way, the tailor will be found a necessary

[1] In his *Journey to Flanders and Holland* Reynolds wrote: "Almost the only demand for considerable works of sculpture arises from the monuments erected to eminent men. It is to be regretted that this circumstance does not produce such an advantage to the art as it might do, if, instead of Westminster Abbey, the custom were once begun of having monuments to departed worth erected in St. Paul's Cathedral. . . . This might be done under the direction of the Royal Academy, who should determine the size of the figures, and where they should be placed, so as to be ornamental to the building" (ii. 341). Thanks largely to Sir Joshua's efforts, this was done. At a meeting of the Academy, 5 May 1791, the president and council were "informed that the dean and chapter of St. Paul's have the intention of permitting monuments to be erected in that cathedral." One of the first was a statue of Reynolds.

[a] Compare the fifth discourse: "If these performances [of Michael Angelo and Raphael in the Vatican] were destroyed, with them would be lost the best part of the reputation of those illustrious painters; for these are justly considered as the greatest efforts of our art which the world can boast" (i. 124).

[b] Compare the fifteenth discourse: "That the young artist may not be seduced from the right path by following what, at first view, he may think the light of reason . . . has been much the object of these discourses" (ii. 192).

[c] Compare the seventh discourse: "No man, for instance, can deny that it seems at first view very reasonable that a statue which is to carry down to posterity the resemblance of an individual should be dressed in the fashion of the times, in the dress which he himself wore. This would certainly be true if the dress were part of the man; but after a time, the dress is only an amusement for an antiquarian; and if it obstructs the general design of the piece, it is to be disregarded by the artist" (i. 211). It will be remembered that when West was painting his *Death of Wolfe*, Reynolds urged him to "adopt the costume of antiquity".

[d] Compare the seventh discourse: "But if he is compelled to exhibit the modern dress, the naked form is entirely hid, and the drapery is already disposed by the skill of the tailor" (i. 212).

person to be consulted [as to] what the exact fashions were in that very year when the person died, that the monument may be correct in the "costume" as the learned call it.[a] We know very well what a difference every year makes in the cut of our clothes.[b]

When it shall be determined by the committee that no monumental figure shall be suffered in St. Paul's but in the modern dress, it will be necessary to add to the committee a certain number of the most ingenious tailors, who shall have a voice in regard to fashion.[c] After the people have been a little accustomed to this naturalness, the Academy will, upon the same principles, proceed a step further and add colour to these statues, which will complete the deception [and] complete the honour of the Royal Academy.[d] This improvement is reserved for this enlightened age,[e] when knowledge is so generally diffused—i.e., when we think for ourselves and dare to reason without prejudices for the opinions of others.[f] We shall soon not leave one stone upon another in the fabric of art. We then rear an edifice not founded on imagination, castles in the air, but on common sense adapted to the meanest capacity, equally comprehended by the ignorant as the learned.[g] My last words are: follow reason, follow nature.[h]

[a] Compare the twelfth discourse (ii. 96), where Sir Joshua uses the word *costume*, but has printed it in italics. Clearly it is to him a "term of art", and therefore to be avoided wherever possible.

[b] Compare the tenth discourse: "He who wishes not to obstruct the artist, and prevent his exhibiting his abilities to their greatest advantage, will certainly not desire a modern dress. The desire of transmitting to posterity the shape of modern dress must be acknowledged to be purchased at a prodigious price, even the price of every thing that is valuable in art. Working in stone is a very serious business; and it seems to be scarce worth while to employ such durable materials in conveying to posterity a fashion of which the longest existence scarce exceeds a year" (ii. 35).

[c] Compare the third discourse: ". . . ill-understood methods which have been practised, to disguise nature, among our dancing-masters, hairdressers, and tailors, in their various schools of deformity" (i. 66).

[d] Compare the tenth discourse: "If the producing of a deception is the summit of this art, let us at once give to statues the addition of colour; which will contribute more towards accomplishing this end than all those artifices which have been introduced and professedly defended on no other principle but that of rendering the work more natural. But as colour is universally rejected, every practice liable to the same objection must fall with it. If the business of sculpture were to administer pleasure to ignorance, or a mere entertainment to the senses, the Venus of Medicis might certainly receive much improvement by colour; but the character of sculpture makes it her duty to afford delight of a different and, perhaps, of a higher kind" (ii. 14).

[e] Reynolds had used this phrase ironically in *Idler* 76, where the connoisseur "lamented that so great a genius as Raphael had not lived in this enlightened age" (ii. 225).

[f] Compare the seventh discourse: "We are creatures of prejudice; we neither can nor ought to eradicate it. . . . I should hope, therefore, that the natural consequence of what has been said would be to excite in you a desire of knowing the principles and conduct of

the great masters of our art, and respect and veneration for them when known" (i. 237, 242).

[g] Compare the seventh discourse: "In the inferior parts of every art, the learned and the ignorant are nearly upon a level" (i. 212).

[h] Compare the last words of the final (fifteenth) discourse: "I should desire that the last words which I should pronounce in this Academy and from this place might be the name of MICHAEL ANGELO." And compare the seventh discourse: "He who thinks nature, in the narrow sense of the word, is alone to be followed, will produce but a scanty entertainment for the imagination. . . . Reason must ultimately determine our choice on every occasion; but this reason may still be exerted ineffectually by applying to taste principles which, though right as far as they go, yet do not reach the object" (i. 210).

APPENDIX III

OTHER NEW REYNOLDS PAPERS

GATHERED together in this appendix are the rest of the Reynolds papers which found their way into Boswell's archives. They consist of Sir Joshua's correspondence with Boswell and Bennet Langton, notes which he made on various subjects, and a few papers which throw light on the sizable fortune he amassed as painter.

The earliest of the letters from Reynolds to Boswell is a brief note which opens up an amusing episode in Boswell's life. In the letter which Boswell wrote to Reynolds on 27 February 1781 (printed on p. 13 of this volume) Boswell hoped "next month to be again in London". His hopes were fulfilled, and his journal shows that on Tuesday, 10 April, he accompanied Johnson and Reynolds in Sir Joshua's coach to the Bishop of St. Asaph's. There he left them, since he had not been invited to dinner, and returned to his own lodgings. Sir Joshua's engagement-book records the dinner at the bishop's, an evening party at Lady Lucan's on the next day, and a dinner at Mrs. Garrick's the following Monday, 16 April. The day after Lady Lucan's party Sir Joshua wrote to Boswell:

DEAR SIR,

When I came home last night, I found a card to remind me of my engagement to dine with Mrs. Garrick next Monday to meet Dr. Johnson. This engagement was made at the Bishop of St. Asaph's on Tuesday, but neglecting to put it down in my book, I thought myself unengaged and gladly accepted the invitation of General Paoli. I must beg therefore you would make my apology to him.

Yours sincerely,

[Thursday] 12 April [1781]. J. REYNOLDS.

APPENDIX III

There is no Boswellian journal for Monday, 16 April, but this note enables us to read Boswell's mind. He had not been asked to dine with Johnson at the Bishop of St. Asaph's; he had not been asked to dine with Johnson at Mrs. Garrick's. Something should be done to remedy an intolerable situation. In Professor Tinker's possession is a letter which Boswell wrote to Mrs. Garrick from General Paoli's on 16 April. After presenting his compliments, he desires to know "at what time he may have the honour of waiting on her", expresses the wish "to pay his respects to Mrs. Garrick, both on account of her own merit, and from his sincere regard for the memory of him 'on whose like we shall not look again', of whose gay and friendly letters Mr. Boswell has a good many, which he fondly preserves as brilliant gems in his literary cabinet". Who could resist so lively a note? Boswell succeeded, of course. He was invited to her house with Dr. Johnson on Friday the twentieth, where he spent what he said was one of the happiest days of his life.

At a famous trial in 1824 the defendant had been called a respectable man, and, when the statement was questioned, the answer was that he kept a gig. The answer delighted Carlyle, who coined the word *giggism*, a synonym for respectability. Sir Joshua would have accepted the statement at its face value. He mentions his coach in this brief note to Boswell:

> DEAR SIR,
>
> I have promised to call on a person in St. Paul's Church-yard this morning at half-past three to see pictures. The coach therefore will be at your door a quarter before three, when I hope you will be ready.
>
> Monday.

Sir Joshua's coach was a symbol of his success in life. Dr. Johnson kept no coach, nor did Goldsmith. But long before he was knighted Mr. Reynolds decided that money thus invested was the best form of advertising. The story is handed down to us by Sir Joshua's pupil, James Northcote, who describes the "chariot, on the panels of which were curiously painted the four seasons of the year in allegorical figures. The wheels were ornamented with carved foliage and gilding; the liveries also of his servants were laced with silver. But having no spare time himself to make a display of this splendour, he insisted on it that his sister Frances should go out with it as much as possible, and let it be seen in the public streets to make a show, which she was much averse to, being a person of great shyness of disposition, as it always attracted the gaze of the populace." Such a grand chariot, Northcote adds, "would give a strong indication of his great success, and by that means tend to increase it."

The next two letters in the correspondence pertain to that "pious negotiation" which is described in full in Boswell's *Life of Johnson*. Boswell had written to the then Lord Chancellor, Thurlow, on 24 June 1784, telling him that Johnson's health was poor and that unless he were sent to a warm climate he would probably be unable to survive the winter. It was a prophetic remark. Boswell suggested that the King might make such a trip possible. Thurlow replied promptly that he would first discuss the matter with Sir Joshua. On 30 June Boswell and Johnson dined at Sir Joshua's and talked about the proposed trip. The next morning Boswell returned to Scotland, never to see Dr. Johnson again. Johnson wrote to him from Ashbourne on 26 July that he was "very feeble and very dejected," intimating that Reynolds was not vigorous in pressing the negotiation. Boswell's letter to Reynolds, here first printed (from Boswell's own copy), is obviously the direct result of Johnson's criticism. It is a good example of Boswell's loyalty to his master and of his tact in handling his friend.

Edinburgh, 3 August 1784.

My dear Sir,

You may believe I am very anxious concerning the success of my "pious negotiation" in favour of Dr. Johnson; and as you kindly undertook to be my successor in the business, after I left London, and the Lord Chancellor wrote to me that he was to confer with you, I trust you will soon be able to give me good accounts. I have had a letter from Dr. Johnson dated at Ashbourne in which he informs me that you had written to the Chancellor but had not received an answer before the Doctor went into the country. I cannot allow myself to think it possible either that Lord Thurlow would neglect so interesting an affair after writing me the strong letter of which you have a copy, or that a still higher Personage would be wanting in liberality after the many professions which he has made to yourself. Dr. Johnson complains chiefly of the asthma in his last letter; so that a warm climate during next winter would, I suppose, be of most essential service to him. He is feeble and dejected; and I am in great concern about him. Let me then entreat you, my dear Sir, to persevere in exerting yourself to obtain for him that Royal Bounty of which he has been flattered with such hopes that it would be mortifying should he be disappointed. I am truly astonished that there has been such a delay. Does it not hurt your generous mind?

Pray let me have the pleasure to hear from you soon; and I beg to have my best compliments presented with all sincerity to Miss Palmer, for whose distress I feel the more, that by a letter from my friend Temple I understand her sister cannot recover.[1] Your delightful temper makes you view human life

[1] Mary Palmer's sister Elizabeth, who had married William Salkeld, died of tuberculosis a few months later. The letter from William Johnson Temple is among the Boswell Papers.

with all its evils as much more agreeable than I do, especially when in the provincial dullness of Edinburgh after the felicity of London. I am with great regard,

My dear Sir Joshua,

Your affectionate humble servant.

The reply to this letter, written a month later, was paraphrased in the *Life of Johnson*, when the biographer sums up his account of the negotiation. The letter from Reynolds is thus part of the raw materials for the *magnum opus*.

London, 2 September 1784.

DEAR SIR,

I had no news to write you relating to our friend Dr. Johnson till today, when the Lord Chancellor called on me to acquaint me with the consequence of his *pious* negotiation. He expressed himself much mortified that it was received not with the warmth he expected. He says he did his utmost, but he fears he has not the art of begging successfully—he would take another opportunity, "but you know," says he, "we must not tease people. However, I would by no means have this journey put off, if necessary to the establishment of his health, on account of the expense. It would be scandalous and shameful that the paltry consideration of money should stand in the way to prevent anything from being done that may any way contribute to the health or amusement of such a man, a man who is an honour to the country." He desired me to inform him that in the mean time he should mortgage his pension to him (the Lord Chancellor) and should draw on him to the amount of five or six hundred pounds. The Chancellor explained the idea of the mortgage to be only this, that he wished this business to be conducted in such a manner as that Dr. Johnson should appear to be under the least possible obligation. I would not neglect acquainting you with this negotiation, which can hardly be called a successful one, though I have just wrote a long letter to Dr. Johnson, and have company with me.

Poor Ramsay is dead, and your humble servant succeeds him as King's Principal Painter. If I had known what a shabby miserable place it is, I would not have asked for it. Besides, as things have turned out, I think a certain person is not worth speaking to, nor speaking of, so I shall conclude.

Yours sincerely,

J. Reynolds

As President of the Royal Academy Sir Joshua had assumed that he would automatically be appointed successor to Allan Ramsay. To his chagrin he had been told that he had to apply for the position. Apparently he considered this beneath his dignity and thought of resigning from the Academy. His friends had persuaded him to swallow his pride, and in his engagement-book for 1 September he wrote: "to attend at the Lord Chamberlain's office to be sworn in Painter to the King, 2 1/2." The next day Johnson wrote to Reynolds, "I am glad that a little favour from the court has intercepted your furious purposes. I could not in any case have approved such public violence of resentment, and should have considered any who encouraged it as rather seeking sport for themselves than honour for you. Resentment gratifies him who intended an injury, and pains him unjustly who did not intend it. But all this is now superfluous." This passage, from a letter now in the Hyde Collection, Boswell did not publish until the second edition of the *Life of Johnson*, after Reynolds had died.

Sir Joshua's bitterness was unconcealed. His new position, he told the Duke of Rutland, was "a place of not so much profit, and near equal dignity, with his Majesty's rat-catcher. . . . This new honour is not likely to elate me very much. I need not make any resolution to behave with the same familiarity as I used to with my old acquaintance." His attitude towards "a certain person", seen in his concluding remark to Boswell, never changed. One of his last letters, an unpublished one to the Bishop of Killaloe, ironically praises the King for his great wisdom.

The last of the new letters in the Boswell–Reynolds correspondence is a note in the handwriting of Mary Palmer.

> Sir Joshua Reynolds and Miss Palmer request the favour of Mr. Boswell's company this evening, if he is not engaged, to play at whist.
>
> Friday morning.

The note can certainly be dated in 1790. On Friday, 8 January, Boswell "went by invitation to Sir Joshua Reynolds', drank tea, and played whist. Metcalfe and Malone were there and we stayed to cold meat." The note was written either on this day or on another Friday six months later, and was preserved because on it are notes for the *Life of Johnson*, which Boswell was revising at the time. One of these reads: "When it was first mentioned at Club that Burke was elected a Memb of Parlt & Sir J Hawk seemed surprised Johnson said now we who know him know he will be one of the first men in this country." This is incorporated into a part of the *Life* which Boswell was revising in the late summer of 1790. "It is very pleasing to me to record, that Johnson's high estimation of the talents of this gentleman was uniform from their early acquaintance. Sir Joshua Reynolds informs me . . ." and then follows the story, the first notation of which was made on the invitation printed above.

Sir Joshua was the first to admit that he was not a good letter-writer. Most of his letters which have survived are brief and business-like, but occasionally he attempted to give his correspondent the news of the day. The letter which follows is more gossipy than most, and is the only letter extant that passed between Reynolds and Bennet Langton. It was discovered by Professor Abbott among the Boswell Papers at Fettercairn House.

Bennet Langton is known today as an intimate of Dr. Johnson and as an original member of the Club. A gentleman of independent means, he had the interests of a scholar, and when in London he sought the companionship of the more thoughtful members of society. From the letter which follows it is clear that Langton had invited Reynolds to visit him in Lincolnshire. Sir Joshua, unable to accept, reports what is happening to members of their circle.

Leicester Fields, 12 September 1782

DEAR SIR,

Though I am but a tardy correspondent, I would not neglect thanking you for your kind invitation, but it is too late in the season to think of any excursion into the country.

I have seen little of Dr. Johnson this year; he is totally absorbed by Mrs. Thrale. I hear however that he is tolerably well and gone to Brighthelmstone with Mrs. Thrale.[1] The papers say that they are going afterwards to Italy, but of this I have heard nothing from authority. If they go, I suppose Miss Burney[2] will be one of the party, as she lives in a manner entirely in that set. I hope you like her last novel, *Cecilia*. Mr. Burke is in raptures and has writ her a complimentary letter. Mr. Fox[3] says it is a wonderful performance.

[1] The fact that Johnson did not go to Brighton with Mrs. Thrale until 7 October supports Sir Joshua's assertion that he is out of touch with his old friend.

[2] Frances Burney (1752–1840), daughter of Sir Joshua's friend Dr. Charles Burney, had become famous when the secret of her authorship of *Evelina* (1778) was revealed. Her second novel, *Cecilia*, had just been published.

[3] Charles James Fox (1749–1806), the statesman.

The Mirror, which you mention, I never saw, but I have heard a good character of it and that some of the first Scotch geniuses were engaged in it. Some of the papers are said to be written by Wedderburn.[1]

I had a letter from Boswell about a fortnight ago, though I think it was more, for it was before his father's death.[2] He writes in good spirits and expresses his longings after London. Mr. Burke often talks of him and appears to have great affection towards him. He says he is by much the most agreeable man he ever saw in all his life.[3]

I hope we shall see you in town early in the season and [that you will] be a regular attender at the Club. I find Adam Smith intends publishing this winter an essay on the reason why imitation pleases.[4] The last day he was there the conversation turned upon that subject. I found it was a subject he had considered with attention. When I saw him afterwards I told him that my notions perfectly agreed with his, that I had wrote a great deal on detached bits of paper, which I would put together and beg him to look over it. He said he could not, for

[1] Alexander Wedderburn, Baron Loughborough (1733–1805), Scottish advocate who later became Lord Chancellor. *The Mirror*, modelled on *The Rambler*, had run from January, 1779, to the end of May, 1780.

[2] Boswell's father had died 30 August. The letter from Boswell to Reynolds has not survived.

[3] Compare the same sentiment quoted above, p. 16, in a letter from Reynolds to Boswell.

[4] Adam Smith (1723–1790) had published *The Wealth of Nations* in 1776. The essay to which Reynolds refers was called "Of the nature of that imitation which takes place in what are called the imitative arts" and was published in *Essays on Philosophical Subjects*.

the reason above mentioned: that he was about finishing an essay on that subject.

I beg my most respectful compliments to Lady Rothes.[1] My niece would join with me, but she is in the west,[2] and my sister is at my house at Richmond,[3] so that I am quite a bachelor.

I am, with the greatest respect,

Yours,

J. REYNOLDS

The subject that Smith and Reynolds had discussed was one dear to Sir Joshua's heart. Among the Reynolds Papers found at Malahide were a few "detached bits of paper" of the sort to which he refers:

Mode

Straight gravel walks are to be removed. A garden, say they, is to be natural. It is to be a landscape.

Without pretending to particular skill in this art, yet I suspect that a true idea of a garden, so far from looking like a landscape or having the appearance of being in the state of nature, ought on the contrary strongly to impress art on the mind and [be] marked with the footsteps of man.

An avenue, or something of regularity of art like it, naturally connects itself and groups with the house which is professedly

[1] Langton's wife.

[2] Mary Palmer had left London for her native Devonshire on 14 August.

[3] Sir Joshua had built a small house at Richmond in 1771, which he used as a base for a day's outing, normally on Sundays. The sister he refers to is Frances Reynolds, the friend of Dr. Johnson.

a formal work of architecture. It is very offensive to my eye to see this formal pile of stone start up from the green sod with nothing about it but an affected irregularity of clumps of shrubs.

Theatrical representation in the same manner has its mode of imitating nature. The best acted scene, the most pathetic and what we call the most natural, will be found on examination very affected, and is really very different from a similar scene in real life.

The idea of imitating nature injudiciously I suspect to be the cause of modern tragedies having given up the chorus, which, I have no doubt, contributed much to the grandeur of the spectacle in the ancient drama.

When Clytemnestra and Iphigenia arrive at Aulis, there is a rich and beautiful scene presented to our imagination of the solicitude and officiousness of the chorus assisting them to descend from the car, whilst others secure the horses from starting.[1]

Quantity is a source of grandeur; a great number of figures enrich the scene and gives that dignity that surely belongs to imperial tragedy. If the mind expands with the grandeur of [the] effect, the great end is answered, and the criticism of naturalness is to be despised.

On Prejudice

In forming the understanding and judgment to acquire the character of what is called a right-headed man, perhaps no part

[1] The reference is to Iphigenia's entrance in *Iphigenia at Aulis* by Euripides.

> of our conduct is more necessary to be watched and attended than our prejudices, the difficulty lying in distinguishing between those which are to be eradicated and those which ought to be received with respect and reverence. It is the power of making this distinction that makes what may truly be called the genius of life. He who has not this power of distinction, which is above all rules, is a wrong-headed man, whatever powers of argument he may possess to prove that he acts from reason and (as he is likely to say himself) is superior to vulgar prejudices.
>
> To apply this to criticism on our art. He would be but a narrow critic who thinks there is but one mode of excellence. Though there are perhaps but few who so confine their view of the art within so narrow a compass, there are likewise very few who see all the excellence and variety of art in its full extent. It is perhaps impossible to avoid a prepossession in favour of that manner which our eyes have been early used to, and though we indulge ourselves in this prejudice, it ought not to exclude our approbation of other manners totally opposite.

Notes of this sort reveal Sir Joshua's philosophical bent. We may be sure that what he has here written was tossed out by him as a subject for discussion by his friends.

There is a brief memorandum which shows, as one might expect, that Reynolds shared Johnson's prejudice in favour of rhyme:

> In regard to determining which to give the preference to, rhyme or blank [verse], if I judge of rhyme from reason I think ill, if from feeling I think I prefer it.

The Boswell Papers contain some items that bear upon what might be called the business side of Sir Joshua's life. Boswell's financial records carry for some years the amount of money he owed to Reynolds, a debt which Sir Joshua eventually "forgave", recalling his similar actions with Johnson and Burke. There is a letter from Wilson Gale Braddyll, M.P., concerning payment for the last of the four portraits Reynolds did for him. And there is a note from Lady Diana Beauclerk to Langton, asking him to find out from Sir Joshua, "without telling him that I made this inquiry," the price he put on the portrait of Mary Beauclerk, her eldest daughter, which had been exhibited in 1780 as *Una and the Lion*. "The case is, that if I find it not beyond what I can afford, I should be very happy to buy it, but dare not mention it till I know, as it may be a great sum." It must have been a great sum, for she never acquired the picture.

But the most revealing of these documents is the draft of what would seem to be the last letter written by Sir Joshua, a letter which helps explain how he became wealthy. It recounts the unhappy story of the part Sir Joshua played in building up Boydell's Shakespeare Gallery.

Late in 1786 Alderman John Boydell was entertaining a group of gentlemen at his home in Hampstead. After dinner, according to the account in Farington's diary, someone remarked that the French "had presented the works of their distinguished authors to the world in a much more respectable manner than the English had done. Shakespeare was mentioned, and several present said they would give a hundred guineas for a fine edition of Shakespeare. Being wound up by the conversation, Alderman Boydell expressed a desire to undertake it, which was warmly encouraged. The next morning Josiah Boydell went to Alderman Boydell's in Cheapside, where he met Romney and Hayley to consult on this scheme. An advertisement was published in a week from this time." This advertisement was for "a most magnificent and accurate edition" of Shakespeare, edited by Steevens and illustrated by the prominent artists of the day. Heading the list of artists was Sir Joshua Reynolds, who in a letter to Boydell dated 8 December objected to the fact that he was not given his correct title, Principal Painter to His Majesty.

APPENDIX III

In a letter to Percy at the end of November, 1786, Malone wrote: "Sir Joshua Reynolds, with whom I dined yesterday . . . has chosen Macbeth for his subject." And early in the new year Sir Joshua reported to the Duke of Rutland: "But the greatest news relating to virtu is Alderman Boydell's scheme of having pictures and prints taken from those pictures of the most interesting scenes of Shakespeare, by which all the painters and engravers find engagements for eight or ten years; he wishes me to do eight pictures, but I have engaged only for one. He has insisted on my taking earnest money, and to my great surprise left upon my table five hundred pounds—to have more as I shall demand."

In his account book, now in the Fitzwilliam Museum in Cambridge, Sir Joshua entered without date: "Mr. Alderman Boydell, for a picture of a Scene in *Macbeth*, not yet begun . . . 500 0 0." And on the fly-leaf of his engagement-book for 1787 is the note: "Mr. Alderman Boydell's cloth: 8 ft. 6 high, 12 ft. long, sight measure." This entry led Leslie and Taylor to say that Reynolds had by the beginning of the year ordered the canvas for his Macbeth. The letter published below indicates that it was Boydell, not Reynolds, who ordered the canvas. It also proves that Leslie and Taylor were not justified in scoffing at the story told by Northcote, which is that Sir Joshua participated in the scheme with reluctance.

The manuscript in the Boswell Papers is in the handwriting of Reynolds and is a draft of a letter which Mary Palmer later copied and sent as from dictation. The draft is erroneously endorsed "The Death of Cardinal Beaufort", another painting done by Reynolds for Boydell. The letter which was actually sent is now in the Folger Library and has never been published. It differs in minor ways from the document here printed. A major difference is that the final four paragraphs of the draft do not appear in the version sent to Boydell. An endorsement to the fair copy dates the letter December, 1791, and a note on the draft reads: "December 15th, State of the Case between Sir J. Reynolds and Mr. Boydell."

[Mary Palmer to John Boydell]

Sir,

My uncle, who from a disorder in his eyes is prevented from writing himself, has dictated the enclosed, which he desires may be communicated to you and Mr. Josiah Boydell.

I am

The letter which Sir Joshua Reynolds has had the honour of receiving from Mr. Boydell, dated December tenth, begins in this manner: "It is so long since [. . .] purchaser," and concludes with desiring to know the price that is put, &c.: "[. . .] become purchaser." To speak so lightly of an engagement in which five hundred pounds was deposited as an earnest that it should be fulfilled appears somewhat extraordinary; it seems to imply what certainly Mr. Boydell can never mean, that he is under no more engagement relating to the picture of Macbeth than to any other unsold picture of his [Sir Joshua's] gallery, that it depended solely on the caprice of the minute whether he would or would not become a purchaser. Mr. Boydell will himself be satisfied that this is not exactly the case, when the whole transaction relating to this picture is laid before him.

This picture [of Macbeth] was undertaken in consequence of the most earnest solicitation on his part, since, after Sir Joshua had twice refused to engage in the business, on the third application Mr. Boydell told him that the success of the whole scheme depended upon his name being seen amongst the list of the performers.

Thus flattered, Sir Joshua said he would give him leave to insert his name as one of the artists who had undertaken to paint for him, and that he would do it if he could; at the same time told him in confidence that his engagement in portraits was such as to make it very doubtful. He recommended to his consideration whether it would be worth his while to give so great a price as he must demand, that though his demand should not be in any proportion to what he got by portrait-painting, yet it would be still more than probably he would think proper to give. To this it was answered that the price was not an object to them, that they would gladly give whatever Sir Joshua should demand, adding that it was necessary they should be able to declare that Sir Joshua was engaged and had received earnest. Bank bills to the amount of five hundred pounds were then laid on the table. To the taking this Sir Joshua expressed great unwillingness, as it seemed to change his lax and conditional promise into a formal obligation. Sir Joshua, however, took the money, but insisted on giving a receipt that the money should be returned if the picture should never be finished.

A few days after this Mr. Boydell, suspecting Sir Joshua's delay, at his own expense sent to Sir Joshua's a canvas measuring nine feet by twelve, the largest that had ever been in his house.

What was to be the price of this picture was never determined. Sir Joshua apprised him that it would be very high [and] desired him to recollect that his fixed prices for portraits were double that of any other painter. To this he was continually answered [that] the price was no object, Sir Joshua should have whatever he demanded, by which Sir Joshua understands whatever he can reasonably demand. Of this neither Mr. Boydell or himself are the judges. Sir Joshua proposes therefore that a select number of artists, or of connoisseurs, with the assistance of some eminent counsellor, shall determine the business by arbitration. The question Sir Joshua apprehends to be whether he can make it appear that he could have got two thousand pounds if he had employed the time in portrait-painting which was employed on that picture (though Sir Joshua demands only fifteen hundred pounds for that picture).

I am far from intending to call in question Mr. Boydell's judgment as a connoisseur in the heroic style of painting. But he must be aware himself that it is very natural for him to depreciate the value of a picture which he wishes to have as cheap as he can. Mr. Boydell says he should be sorry to see Sir Joshua the only painter that does not co-operate with him, by giving up part of their profit to the great national object of introducing a taste for historical painting.

One would wish to ask if any profit is like to proceed from this scheme. If there is, it is but reasonable that the co-operators with Mr. Boydell ought to have a share besides that of the honour of being patrons and promoters or co-operators of this public good. It is supposed that Mr. Boydell will acquire a considerable fortune by his patronage of the arts, and as he acknowledged that the living painters have been his co-adjutors, it seems but reasonable they should have a share of the profit.

As for the co-operation of the artists with Mr. Boydell in this national scheme, if those artists have been persuaded by Mr. Boydell to work for him at an underrate, to act justly

Mr. Boydell ought to allow them a share of the profit which it is supposed he will gain by this scheme. It is certainly unreasonable to make the artists themselves be at the expense, whilst Mr. Boydell runs away both with the honour and profit.

Sir Joshua is therefore humbly of opinion that Mr. Boydell is not entirely at liberty whether he will or will not become a purchaser of the picture in question, but is obliged to take it at a reasonable price. What price shall be deemed reasonable, neither Mr. Boydell nor Sir Joshua are proper judges in their own causes.

For a sequel to the story we must look elsewhere. In their monumental catalogue of Sir Joshua's paintings Graves and Cronin print the following account, excerpted from a newspaper of January, 1792: "Sir Joshua Reynolds is again recovering. He has regained the use of one eye, enough at least to see that he is not likely to have fair play in the *Shakespeare Gallery*, without the aid of *John Doe*! A curious pictorial case will soon be brought upon canvas in Westminster Hall, SIR JOSHUA REYNOLDS on the part of Macbeth & Co. Plaintiff, and Mr. Alderman BOYDELL and firm, Defendants. The action is to recover 1,500 guineas for a picture, said to be painted per order, for the *Shakespeare Gallery*." In spite of this account, written while Reynolds was on his death-bed, the matter was settled as Sir Joshua recommended. It was referred to a committee which included Sir George Beaumont, Sir Abraham Hume, William Lock, John Thomas Batt, and the Bishop of Peterborough, and the committee fixed the price at a thousand pounds. It is melancholy to add that when financial difficulties later forced Boydell to sell the painting at auction, it fetched only three hundred and sixty guineas. Meanwhile, before it had been paid for, Sir Joshua died. The document here printed may be considered the last business transaction in the life of a successful painter.

REFERENCES TO SOURCES

CUE TITLES:

BP: *The Private Papers of James Boswell . . . in the Collection of Lt.-Col. Ralph H. Isham*, ed. Geoffrey Scott and Frederick A. Pottle, 1928–1934.

Farington: Volume one of *The Farington Diary*, ed. James Greig, London, 1923.

Johns. Misc.: *Johnsonian Miscellanies*, ed. G. B. Hill, Oxford, 1897.

Leslie and Taylor: *Life and Times of Sir Joshua Reynolds* by Charles Robert Leslie and Tom Taylor, London, 1865.

Letters: *Letters of Sir Joshua Reynolds*, ed. F. W. Hilles, Cambridge, 1929.

Life: Boswell's *Life of Johnson*, ed. G. B. Hill and L. F. Powell, Oxford, 1934–1950.

Northcote: *The Life of Sir Joshua Reynolds* by James Northcote, London, 1818 (the second edition).

Prior's *Goldsmith*: *The Life of Oliver Goldsmith* by James Prior, London, 1837.

Thraliana: *Thraliana, The Diary of Mrs. Hester Lynch Thrale*, ed. Katharine C. Balderston, Oxford, 1942.

Works: *The Works of Sir Joshua Reynolds, to which is prefixed an Account of the Life and Writings of the Author by Edmond Malone*, London, 1798 (the second edition).

Sir Joshua's engagement-books are in the Royal Academy.

Page ix. Boswell's comment on Reynolds's portrait: BP, xviii. 143 (Journal 1 September 1792).

Malone on Burke's obituary: *Works*, i. p. cxix.

Boswell takes notes: Original letter in Boswell Papers to Erskine, 6 March 1793.

Northcote on Goldsmith's portrait: Northcote, i. 326.

REFERENCES TO SOURCES

Page x. Reynolds on his writing: *Letters*, 20.

Boswell on Johnson's portrait: *Life*, i. 392 (16 May 1763).

Hawkins on Johnson's portrait: *Johns. Misc.* ii. 9.

Walpole on Garrick's portrait: Horace Walpole's *Anecdotes of Painting in England*, ed. F. W. Hilles and Philip B. Daghlian, New Haven, 1937, 61.

Northcote on Garrick's portrait: Northcote, ii. 36 *n*.

Page xi. Hannah More on Dialogues: Leslie and Taylor, ii. 260.

Malone on Gibbon's portrait: Sir James Prior's *Life of Malone*, London, 1860, 382.

Page xiii. "Request of friends": Pope's *Epistle to Arbuthnot*, line 44.

"Already appeared in print": *Letters*, 194–199; *Letters of James Boswell*, ed. C. B. Tinker, Oxford, 1924, 319, 327.

Page xiv. "Close study of the characters . . . ": Farington, 262.

"Amusement for an antiquarian": Seventh discourse, *Works*, i. 212.

Page 1. "A few minutes": *Memoirs of Benjamin Robert Haydon*, London, 1926, 795.

"Lapidary inscriptions": *Life*, ii. 407 (following 5 December 1775).

"Contemporary journalist": Northcote, ii. 290.

Burke's obituary: *Works*, i. pp. cxix–cxxiv.

Page 3. "Reading, if it can be made . . .": Seventh discourse, *Works*, i. 191.

"A very learned and thinking man": *Works*, i. p. xcviii *n*.

Page 4. "Romulus": *Johns. Misc.* i. 230.

Ἄναξ ἀνδρῶν: *Life*, i. 47 (1719–1725).

"No book goes rapidly . . .": *Thraliana*, 80.

"Gentle, complying, and bland": Goldsmith's *Retaliation*.

Page 5. "My Lady O'Brien": Leslie and Taylor, i. 218 *n*.5.

"Mediterranean friends": BP, x. 155 (Journal 27 March 1775).

"Gloomy tyrant": Farington, 262.

"Strong turn for humour": Leslie and Taylor, ii. 638 *n*.

"Uncommon flow of spirits": *Memoirs of Reynolds* by Joseph Farington, London, 1819, 260.

"Activity and placid disposition": BP, xvii. 47 (Journal 14 October 1787).

Page 6. Madame d'Arblay: *Memoirs of Dr. Burney*, London, 1832, ii. 365.

Page 8. "Sinuous climber": Louis Kronenberger in the *Portable Johnson and Boswell*, Viking Press, New York, 1947, 19. The most prejudiced modern characterisation appears in R. H. Wilenski's *English Painting*, London, 1933.

"Too much merit": *Works*, i. p. cxxiii.

*n.*2: Alexander Gilchrist's *Life of Blake*, London, 1880, i. 307.

Page 9. "Knight of Plympton": *Life*, iv. 432.

Parr to Boswell: unpublished letter in Boswell Papers.

Northcote's letter: William T. Whitley's *Artists and their Friends in England*, London, 1928, ii. 296. The original letter is in the Royal Academy.

Mrs. Thrale: *Thraliana*, 473, 728.

Page 10. Reynolds on marriage: BP, xvii. 88 (Journal 29 March 1788).

Page 11. Burke to Malone: *Works*, i. p. xcvii.

Page 13. Boswell's journal: BP, xvii. 52, 56, 57, 68, 130; xvi. 215 (Journal 28 July 1786, 31 October 1787, 26 and 27 November 1787, 14 February 1788; letter to Mrs. Boswell 28 November 1788).

Page 14. *n.*2: BP, x. 206 (Journal 11 April 1775).

Page 15. *n.*1: BP, xiv. 255 (Letters from Margaret Stuart 27 February 1780).

*n.*2: *Letters*, 119.

Page 17. Mary Palmer: Farington, 96.

Page 18. Malone: *Works*, i. p. cix.

Page 19. Mrs. Piozzi to Percy: *Thraliana*, 835.

Page 21. *n.*1: Sir Robert Edgcumbe in Graves and Cronin's *History of the Works of Sir Joshua Reynolds*, London, 1901, p. 1691.

Page 22. *n.*1: Northcote, i. 19.

Page 23. Obituary of Boswell: William T. Whitley's *Artists and their Friends in England*, London, 1928, ii. 174.
"Serious intentions": Farington, 95.
"Teem with point": *Life*, iii. 260 (10 April 1778).
*n.*1: Johnson's *Lives of the English Poets*, ed. G. B. Hill, Oxford, 1905, iii. 178 *n.*2.

Page 24. Boswell on Reynolds's conversation: BP, vi. 62 (Journal 5 June 1784).
"This eminent man": BP, xvi. 122 (Journal 28 August 1785).

Page 25. "A venerable aged lady": *Memoirs of Benjamin Robert Haydon*, London, 1926, 793.

Page 26. "Sir Joshua's well-known portrait": Prior's *Goldsmith*, ii. 310, 380, 333. Northcote, i. 326.
"No conceit or affectation": The letter from Northcote, dated 21 September 1771, is in the Royal Academy.
"Singled out by a journalist": Noted by Professor R. S. Crane in *Life*, iii. 502.

Page 27. Beauclerk: Francis Hardy's *Memoirs of the Earl of Charlemont*, London, 1812, i. 350.

Page 28. Goldsmith to Reynolds: *Letters of Oliver Goldsmith*, ed. Balderston, Cambridge, 1928, 93.
"Hostile view": *Thraliana*, 80.

Page 29. Johnson defends Goldsmith: Northcote, i. 327.
Boswell calls on Percy: BP, x. 157 (Journal 28 March 1775).
"Expressed his approbation": *Dr. Campbell's Diary*, ed. James L. Clifford, Cambridge, 1947, 77.

Page 30. Maurice Goldsmith to Percy: Katharine C. Balderston's *History and Sources of Percy's Memoir*, Cambridge, 1926, 19.
"Original letter": Katharine C. Balderston's *History and Sources of Percy's Memoir*, Cambridge, 1926, 59. *Percy–Malone Correspondence*, ed. Arthur Tillotson, University, Louisiana, 1944, 32, 49.

Page 31. "Loan of ten pounds": Northcote, i. 288.

Page 32. "Talk like WHALES": *Life*, ii. 231 (27 April 1773).
"Second-hand coat": Prior's *Goldsmith*, i. 215. *Autobiography of Miss Cornelia Knight*, London, 1861, i. 11.

Page 33. "Teaching his dog to beg": Prior's *Goldsmith*, ii. 33.
Goldsmith and the apothecary: Prior's *Goldsmith*, ii. 105.
"Kicking a bundle": Prior's *Goldsmith*, ii. 353.

Page 34. "He told students of art": *Works*, i. 82.

Page 35. Boswell's sketch of Goldsmith: *Life*, i. 411–415 (following 25 June 1763).
"Among those who objected": Prior's *Goldsmith*, i. 442–446.
"Footnote to the *Life*": *Life*, i. 412 *n.* (following 25 June 1763).

Page 36. "Agreeable trifling": Goldsmith's *Works* (*Polite Learning in Europe*), ed. J. W. M. Gibbs, London, 1885, iii. 514.
Boswellian anecdote: *Life*, i. 414 (following 25 June 1763). Compare Prior's *Goldsmith*, ii. 291.

Page 37. Mrs. Primrose: *Vicar of Wakefield*, chap. XII.
"Irascible as a hornet": *Life*, v. 97 *n.*3 (*Tour to Hebrides*, note on 24 August 1773).

Page 38. "Chaos of thought and passion": Pope's *Essay on Man*, II. 13.

Page 40. *n.*1: *Letters*, 87.

Page 41. *n.*2: *Life*, i. 412 *n.* (following 25 June 1763).

Page 43. *n.*1: *Life*, i. 411 (following 25 June 1763).
*n.*2: *Life*, ii. 231; i. 423 (27 April 1773; 6 July 1763).

Page 44. *n.*1: *Life*, ii. 186 (11 April 1772).
*n.*2: *Life*, ii. 167, 252 (19 September 1777; 9 April 1778).
*n.*3: *Life*, ii. 236 (30 April 1773).

Page 45. *n.*1: *Letters of Goldsmith*, ed. Balderston, Cambridge, 1928, 29.

Page 46. *n.*1: Northcote, i. 248.

Page 47. *n.*1: Prior's *Goldsmith*, ii. 127.

Page 48. *n.*1: *Life*, i. 417 (1 July 1763).
*n.*2: Goldsmith's *Works*, ed. J. W. M. Gibbs, London, 1886, v. 199.

Page 49. *n.*2: *Life*, iv. 175 *n.* (23 March 1783).

Page 50. *n.*1: *Life*, iii. 253 (9 April 1778).

Page 51. *n.*1: *Mamamouchi*, London, 1675, 7.

Page 52. *n.*1: *Life*, iv. 29 (1780).

Page 53. *n.*1: Northcote, i. 326.

Page 55. First meeting of Johnson and Reynolds: *Life*, i. 244 (1752).

Page 56. "The many mistakes": *The French Journals of Mrs. Thrale and Dr. Johnson*, ed. M. Tyson and H. Guppy, Manchester, 1932, 45.
Boswell calls on Mrs. Lewis: BP, xvi. 194 (Journal 14 June 1786).
Reynolds annoyed at Johnson's visits: Northcote, i. 79.

Page 57. "Writ by an angel": F. W. Hilles's *Literary Career of Sir Joshua Reynolds*, Cambridge, 1936, 152.
"Qualified my mind": *Works*, i. p. xxx.
"When Reynolds tells me": *Johns. Misc.* i. 225.
"I am always proud": *Life*, iv. 368 (2 October 1784).
Johnson to Reynolds: *Life*, i. 486 (August 1764).
"Two have . . . been known to survive": *Letters*, 57, 75.
Fanny Burney: *Diary of Madame d'Arblay*, ed. Dobson, London, 1904, ii. 124.
"According to Boswell": *Life*, iv. 109 (May 1781).

Page 58. "Goldy": *Life*, ii. 258 (7 May 1773).
"Like a Quaker": William Hazlitt's *Conversations of James Northcote*, London, 1830, 289.

Page 59. "Anything like friction": *Dr. Campbell's Diary*, ed. Clifford, Cambridge, 1947, 54; *Life*, ii. 292; iii. 329 (21 January 1775; 28 April 1778).
Boswell and Johnson in coach: BP, vi. 56 (Journal 3 June 1784).

Page 60. Reynolds to Rutland: *Letters*, 140. Compare BP, vi. 171 (Journal 22 September 1785).
Footnote in second edition: p. 9.

Page 62. "Accordingly in the *Life*": *Life*, i. 144 (1739).
"Note that Pope wrote": *Life*, i. 143 (1739).
"Wrote some anecdotes": BP, xvi. 167 (Journal 20 February 1786).
"Pointed out elsewhere": F. W. Hilles's *Literary Career of Sir Joshua Reynolds*, Cambridge, 1936, 167–172.

Page 64. "Undoubtedly admirable": *Life*, iii. 332 (29 April 1778).

Page 65. "I have transcribed": Leslie and Taylor, ii. 454.

Page 68. *n*.1: *Johns. Misc.* ii. 156, 203.
n.2: *Life*, iv. 253 (4 December 1783).

Page 69. *n*.1: Sir James Prior's *Life of Malone*, London, 1860, 92.

Page 70. *n*.1: *Life*, iv. 226, 513 (29 May 1783).

Page 71. *n*.1: *Johns. Misc.* ii. 278.

Page 72. *n*.1: *Boswell's London Journal*, 1762–1763, ed. Pottle, London, 1950, 282; *Life*, ii. 327 (Journal 25 June 1763; *Life* 28 March 1775).
n.2: *Life*, ii. 64 (summer 1768).

Page 75. *n*.1: *Johns. Misc.* ii. 262.

Page 79. *n*.1: *Life*, iv. 15 (1780).
n.2: *Life*, iv. 186 (between 30 March and 10 April 1783).

Page 80. *n*.1: *Johns. Misc.* ii. 127, 152.

Page 81. Boswell's version: *Life*, iii. 386 (24 April 1779).

Page 82. "Sir Joshua told Malone": Sir James Prior's *Life of Malone*, London, 1860, 416.

Page 83. Foote's *bon mot*: *Johnsoniana . . . together with Choice Sentences of Publilius Syrus*, London, 1776, 50.

Page 84. Nollekens and Garrick: Northcote, ii. 36.
Northcote and Garrick: Northcote, i. 234.
Malone and Garrick: Prior's *Life of Malone*, 376.
Fitzgerald: Percy Fitzgerald's *Life of David Garrick*, London, 1868, ii. 424.

Page 89. Jekyll to Ellis: from the original in the possession of F. W. Hilles.

Page 90. Miss Hawkins: *Gossip about Dr. Johnson and Others*, ed. Francis H. Skrine, London, 1926, 79.

Boswell's journal: BP, xviii. 94 (Journal 9 September 1790).

"Johnson considered Garrick . . . his *property*": *Life*, iii. 312 (17 April 1778).

"Tyers's apt statement": *Life*, iii. 307 (17 April 1778).

Page 91. R. Brimley Johnson: *Johnson and Garrick* (Cayme Press Pamphlet no. 9), Kensington, 1927, 6.

Page 95. *n.*1: *Life*, iv. 315 (June 1784).

Page 107. Reynolds on Shakespeare: F. W. Hilles's *Literary Career of Sir Joshua Reynolds, Cambridge*, 1936. 27–29, 98–105.

Boswell to Malone: *Letters of James Boswell*, ed. C. B. Tinker, Oxford, 1924, 406.

Burke to Malone: Leslie and Taylor, ii. 638 *n.*

Page 121. *n.*1: William Mason: Mason's *Memoirs of Thomas Gray*, York, 1778, ii. 34 (note to Letter IX).

Page 123. "Words of Malone": *Works*, i. p. ciii.

Farington's opinion: Farington, 136.

Reynolds on Burke's *Reflections*: *Works*, i. p. cii.

Quotation from fifteenth discourse: *Works*, ii. 215, 213.

*n.*1: Alexander Gilchrist's *Life of Blake*, London, 1880, i. 95.

Page 124. Malone on French Revolution: *Works*, ii. 414 *n.*

Page 125. Reynolds and Barry: Northcote, ii. 147, 146.

Page 149. Reynolds's coach: Stephen Gwynn's *Memorials of an Eighteenth Century Painter*, London, 1898, 245.

Page 152. Johnson to Reynolds: *Life*, iv. 366 (2 September 1784).

Page 153. Reynolds to Rutland: *Letters*, 112.

Boswell and whist: BP, xviii. 16, 81 (Journal 8 January, 23 July 1790).

Note on Burke: *Life*, ii. 450 (20 March 1776).

REFERENCES TO SOURCES

Page 159. Boydell's dinner: Farington, 237
Sir Joshua to Boydell: *Letters*, 170.

Page 160. Malone to Percy: *Percy–Malone Correspondence*, ed. Arthur Tillotson, University, Louisiana, 1944, 47.
Sir Joshua to Rutland: *Letters*, 174.
Negotiations with Boydell: Leslie and Taylor, ii. 502.

Page 164. Excerpt from newspaper: Graves and Cronin's *History of the Works of Sir Joshua Reynolds*, London, 1901, p. 1171.

INDEX

This is for the most part an index of proper names. The following abbreviations have been employed: J.R. (Sir Joshua Reynolds), J.B. (James Boswell), S.J. (Samuel Johnson), O.G. (Oliver Goldsmith), D.G. (David Garrick), *Life* (Boswell's *Life of Johnson*).

INDEX

INDEX

LEICESTER SQUARE